K-3 SCIENCE ACTIVITIES KIT

K-3 SCIENCE ACTIVITIES KIT

Carol A. Poppe

Nancy A. Van Matre

Illustrated by

Nancy A. Van Matre

**THE CENTER FOR APPLIED
RESEARCH IN EDUCATION**
West Nyack, New York 10995

Library of Congress Cataloging-in-Publication Data

Poppe, Carol A.
    K-3 science activities kit / Carol A. Poppe, Nancy A. Van Matre;
illustrated by Nancy A. Van Matre.
    p.   cm.
    ISBN 0-87628-477-2
    1. Science—Study and teaching (Primary) 2. Independent study.
3. Creative activities and seatwork. I. Van Matre, Nancy A.
II. Title. III. Title: K-three science activities kit.
LB1532.P66 1988
372.3′5044—dc19   87-33411
                                          CIP

ISBN 0-87628-477-2

**THE CENTER FOR APPLIED
RESEARCH IN EDUCATION**
BUSINESS & PROFESSIONAL DIVISION
A division of Simon & Schuster
West Nyack, New York 10995

Printed in the United States of America

We wish to dedicate this book

To our Parents,
Our first teachers.

Clarence, Otha, Alwin, Marie

And...

Our families, who continue to teach us.

Jason

John

Nancy

Molly

Jenny

Doug

Mike

About the Authors

Carol A. Poppe received her B.A. degree from Ohio University and has taken several graduate courses at Oakland University and Siena Heights College. Mrs. Poppe has 22 years of teaching experience at the first- and second-grade levels. With Nancy Van Matre, she co-authored *Science Learning Centers for the Primary Grades* (The Center for Applied Research in Education, Inc. 1985).

Nancy A. Van Matre received her B.A. and her M.A. degrees in Reading Education from Eastern Michigan University. She has been actively teaching grades one through three since 1975.

Both authors have presented several learning center workshops for other educators in Michigan and Ohio and are currently teaching first grade in the Clinton Community Schools in Clinton, Michigan. Learning center activities have been an integral part of their daily classroom schedules since 1976.

About This Book

     K-3 Science Teacher's Activities Kit is designed to provide the primary, gifted and talented, or resource room teacher with activities to extend the science curriculum in a stimulating and high-interest manner. The ideas and activities presented in this resource are appropriate for students in kindergarten through third grade at all developmental levels.

     Each set of directions for the 40 activities combines illustrations with simple sentences to enable virtually every child to complete the activities independently.

     Management suggestions are given if you wish to use the science unit activities in a learning center. Specific techniques are presented to help adapt your classroom environment for these science activities.

     A convenient Skills Chart is provided, which clearly shows the critical thinking skills required for each science activity in the book.

     Innovative approaches that encourage parent involvement, both in the classroom and at home, are also given.

     This sourcebook provides a complete teaching package of five science units that may be used in non-sequential order. Each unit is based on an appropriate theme, including:

- Weather
- Nutrition
- Birds
- Trees
- Pets

     Each science unit contains file folder directions, ready-to-use ideas, and reproducible materials for eight different science activities related to the science unit theme. These are designed to give the child an opportunity to explore science activities independently. Special features of each science unit are:

1. An appealing, reproducible unit opener that can be used for bulletin boards or file covers, for example.
2. A parent letter explaining the science unit activities.

3. A reproducible learning center marker for each student who uses the science unit activities at learning centers.

4. A master list of the eight science activities in each unit that you can use as a convenient reference in a lesson planbook, materials storage box, and so on.

5. Eight theme-related science activities for each unit that also reinforce skills in the following areas: science, math, art, spelling, handwriting, and reading.

6. In each Science Unit one of the eight activities is "open ended" to accommodate a teacher's choice. The teacher chooses any appropriate grade level skill he or she wishes to emphasize, then adapts it for the activity. Some ideas are: reviewing spelling, reading or scientific vocabulary, reinforcing an appropriate math level skill, and so on.

7. Teacher's directions for each activity that include:
   - Content areas used
   - Skills used
   - Materials needed
   - Materials preparation
   - Bibliography of background sources
   - Directions for file folders

The activities may be used at learning centers or individual interest stations. They are uniquely organized to save preparation time, effort, and expense. Once constructed, the file folder directions for the activities may become part of your permanent collection of science units. Management techniques are clearly provided for this purpose.

In addition, each science unit contains enrichment activities, including a whole group activity. Practical teacher suggestions are given for using reproducible enrichment activity pages for boardwork, seatwork, vocabulary development, home study, evaluation, awards, and so on.

Each science unit's enrichment activities include:

1. A group activity that can be done by the entire class.
2. A home study activity to encourage child-parent participation.
3. Illustrated awards forms for home study and recognition of progress.
4. Illustrated evaluation forms for each science unit.
5. Reproducible enrichment activity pages that include creative writing, vocabulary development, and coordination development.
6. Practical suggestions for students' use of the enrichment activity pages.

We hope you and your students will enjoy working with these activities. You should find that as they develop an interest in science, they are also increasing their ability to work independently.

Carol A. Poppe
Nancy Van Matre

To the Teacher

Constructing the Science Activity Direction File Folders:
The directions for each of the Science Activities in this book are designed to fit on 12″ by 18″ file folders. Brightly colored file folders are attractive for this purpose. A glue stick works well for mounting the direction pages. Crayons or water-base marking pens may be used to color the illustrations and numbers. (Prior to mounting any directions, be sure the other side of the page has been duplicated for future use.)

How to make the direction file folder:

1. Glue the Teacher Directions to the back of the file folder. (This visual aid is helpful to the teacher in organizing the necessary materials for the Science Activity.)
2. Glue the Directions for File Folder Activities to the adjacent back side of the file folder.

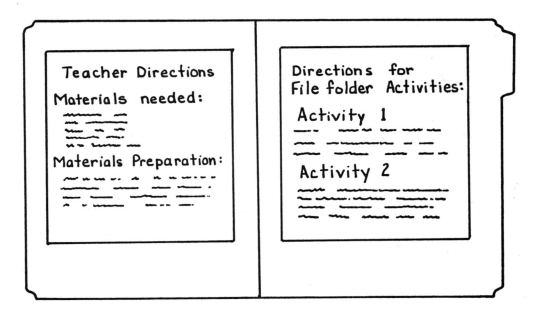

3. Color the pictures on the student File Folder Directions page.

4. Color the numbers orange on the student File Folder Directions page. (Use the same format for all of the file folders.)

5. Glue the student "File Folder Directions" page to the front of the file folder.

6. Laminate or use clear Con-Tact paper to cover all of the direction file folders.

Optional ideas for making direction file folders:

1. Additional theme pictures from magazines, catalogs, etc. may be glued to the front side of the file folder (adjacent to the student "File Folder Directions" page).

2. A 10″ by 13″ envelope with a student activity page mounted on it may be attached to the front side of the file folder (adjacent to the student "File Folder Directions" page). The envelope is used as a container for the student activity page.

Direction file folder tip for the non-reader or beginning reader:

1. Make a set of corresponding "File Folder Directions" numbers on 1″ squares of orange construction paper with a black marking pen. Staple or tape these numbers to the student activity page container, books, tape recorder, games, etc. at the learning center. The numbers assist the student with less developed reading skills to complete the activities in sequential order.

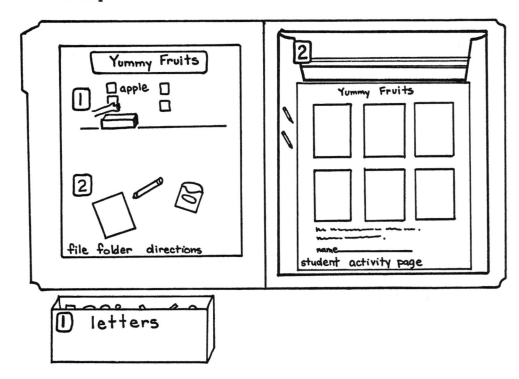

Storing the science units:

Once constructed, the Direction for File Folders Activities may become part of a permanent collection of science units. It is helpful to keep the direction file folders and materials for each science unit in a large cardboard storage box. An ideal size is 27″ by 16″ by 12″ high with a lid (most discount stores have these boxes in flat packages). The same size boxes can be easily labeled, carried, and stacked utilizing a minimum amount of floor space. The master science activities list may be taped inside the lid for easy reference.

Contents

Unit 2: Nutrition   51

Unit 3: Birds 99

Birds Activities List 103

Birds Enrichment Activities 131

Teacher's Suggestions for Birds Enrichment Activities 132

Group Activities 133

Letter to Parents 137

Home Study 139

Unit 4: Trees 147

SCIENCE UNITS

Unit 1 Weather

Unit 2 Nutrition

Unit 3 Birds

Unit 4 Trees

Unit 5 Pets

Unit 1
WEATHER

UP, UP AND AWAY!

Date _____

Dear Parent,

     Our class will be conducting many weather-related experiments in our study of static electricity, water vapor, evaporation, wind, and rainbows.

     Please encourage your child to listen to weather forecasts on the radio and television. He or she is welcome to bring weather maps, books, and charts to class during the next two weeks.

     As a weather forecasting activity, your child will record temperatures and weather symbols for several cities on a map. In addition, he or she will read thermometers and a barometer and record his or her readings. It would be helpful for your child to practice these skills at home.

     Your child will need a 9-inch aluminum foil pie pan to make a lightning mobile. Please send it as soon as possible.

     As a group weather activity, we will launch helium-filled balloons on _____at _____. You
                           day   *time*
are welcome to watch this exciting event.

     Thank you for your continued support.

Sincerely,

_____
Your child's teacher

- -

If you would be willing to help with the balloon launch, please sign _____and return by _____. I will contact you for definite arrangements.

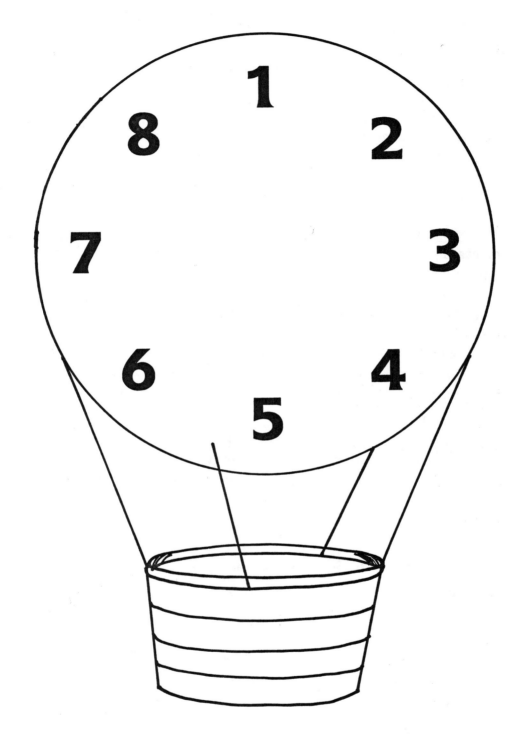

Weather Center Marker

WEATHER CENTER MARKER

A learning center marker is provided for students using the science unit activities at learning centers. (Refer to p. 246)

Distribute copies of the preceding balloon marker to the students. The students can cut out their markers and place them ηear the Weather Learning Centers.

WEATHER ACTIVITIES LIST

These activities relate to various aspects of weather, including weather forecasting, weather experiments, and the seasons. Each is described in detail later.

1. **Weather Forecasting Activity** (A bulletin board is used with this activity)

   Content areas: Science, reading, math

   Skills: Predicting, observing, measuring (temperature, atmospheric pressure), map reading, communication, experimenting

   Activities:

   a. Record today's temperatures and weather symbols for the cities shown on the Weather Map student activity page.
   b. Take weather readings for your area and record them on the My Forecast student activity page.
   Make forecasts.

2. **Wind Activity**

   Content areas: Science, art, reading

   Skills: Observing, experimenting, creating, map reading, compass reading, fine-motor coordination

   Activities:

   a. The student will make a wind vane.
   b. The student will make a pinwheel.
   c. The student will conduct wind experiments outdoors.

3. Snow Activity (Open-ended activity)

Content areas: Handwriting, teacher's choice, reading

Skills: Fine-motor coordination, using reference materials, teacher's choice

Activities:

a. Make a "Blizzard Bag."

b. Write words on snowballs, cut them out, and place them in a bag.

4. Rain Activity

Content areas: Science, handwriting

Skills: Communication, observing, experimenting, fine-motor coordination

Activities:

a. Conduct two water-cycle experiments.

b. Complete water-cycle sentences on the Water Cycle student activity page.

5. Clouds Activity

Content areas: Reading, art, science

Skills: Listening, creating, fine-motor coordination, classifying

Activities:

a. Listen to book about clouds.

b. Write cloud names on the Clouds student activity page.

c. Fingerpaint clouds.

6. Lightning Activity

Content areas: Science, art

Skills: Creating, fine-motor coordination, experimenting, measuring, predicting

Activities:

a. Conduct static electricity experiment.

b. Make a lightning mobile.

7. Rainbows Activity

Content areas: Science, art

Skills: Creating, experimenting, observing

Activities:

a. Conduct two rainbow experiments.
b. Paint a rainbow.

8. Seasons Activity

Content areas: Handwriting, art, science

Skills: Creating, communicating, fine-motor coordination, creative writing

Activities:

a. Color the "Seasons of the Earth" book cover.
b. Write, illustrate, and assemble the book.

TEACHER'S DIRECTIONS FOR THE WEATHER FORECASTING ACTIVITY

Content areas: Science, reading, math

Skills: Predicting, observing, measuring (temperature, atmospheric pressure), map reading, communication, experimenting

Materials needed:

Bulletin board	Calendar
Pencil	Large map of the United States
Crayons	Copies of student activity pages
Barometer	Water-based marking pens
Clock	Fahrenheit or Celsius thermometers (one indoor and one outdoor)

Materials preparation:

1. Prepare a bulletin board with a map of the United States and a weather symbol chart as pictured on the "Weather Map" student activity page 12. Laminate the map or cover it with clear Con-Tact paper.
2. Using a copy of the "Weather Map" student activity page 12, make a daily chart. Use the chart to record the temperatures and weather symbols (sunny, cloudy, rainy, snowy) for the cities indicated on the map.
3. Be sure the student is able to
   a. Read Fahrenheit or Celsius thermometers and record temperatures.
   b. Read barometers and record atmospheric pressure.
   c. Define precipitation, wind, season, and forecast.
4. Some good books to establish weather forecasting background are: Burnett, R. Will, Lehr, Paul E., and Zim, Herbert S., *Weather,* Western Publishing Co., Inc., Golden Press, New York, 1975; Lutgens, Frederick K. and Tarbuck, Edward J. *The Atmosphere,* Prentice-Hall, Inc., Englewood Cliffs, N. J., 1979; May, Julian, *What Will The Weather Be?,* Creative Educational Society, Mankato, Minn., 1972; Sattler, Helen R., *Nature's Weather Forecasts,* Thomas Nelson Inc., New York, 1978.

DIRECTIONS FOR FILE FOLDER ACTIVITIES

Activity 1

1. The student, referring to the daily chart, uses marking pens to record the daily temperatures and weather symbols for the cities shown on the map.
2. The student uses the "Weather Map" student activity page to
   a. Copy the temperatures and weather symbols from the map on the bulletin board.
   b. Record the temperature in Fahrenheit or Celsius on the first line under each thermometer.
   c. Color each thermometer red up to the line that corresponds with the temperature recorded on the line below.
   d. Draw the proper weather symbol on the second line under each thermometer.

Activity 2

The student uses the "My Forecast" student activity page to

1. Record the information requested.
2. Draw a picture of today's forecast and tomorrow's forecast in the appropriate box.

Weather Forecasting

1 Write today's temperatures and signs for each city on the map. Record them on your worksheet.

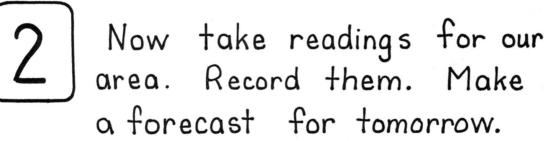

2 Now take readings for our area. Record them. Make a forecast for tomorrow.

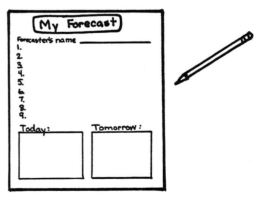

File Folder Directions

Weather Map

name _____ date _____

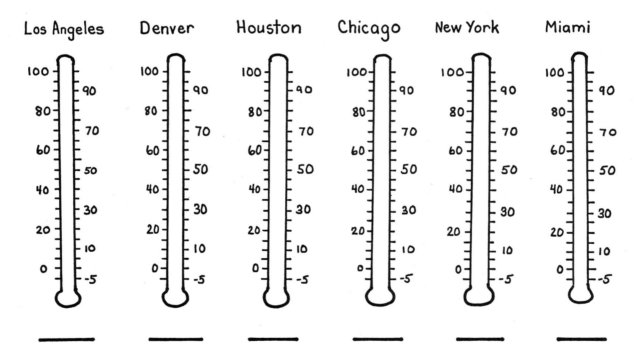

Los Angeles   Denver   Houston   Chicago   New York   Miami

Student Activity Page

My Forecast

Forecaster's name _____

1. Today is _____ _____ ____ ____
   day of week   month   date year

2. Season: _____

3. Time: _____

4. Outdoor temperature _____

5. Indoor temperature _____

6. Sky : _____

7. Precipitation _____

8. Wind _____

9. Barometric Pressure _____

Today's Forecast:

Tomorrow's Forecast:

Student Activity Page

TEACHER'S DIRECTIONS FOR THE WIND ACTIVITY

Content areas: Science, art, reading

Skills: Observing, creating, fine-motor coordination, map reading, experimenting, compass reading

Materials needed:

Teacher-made wind vane pattern	Compass
Copies of student activity page	Ruler
One pencil with eraser per student	Scissors
One brass fastener per student	One straight pin per student
One 9-inch paper plate per student	One 12-inch piece of string per student

Materials preparation:

1. Be sure the students know how to use a compass.
2. Arrange an outdoor location in which the students can conduct their wind vane and pinwheel experiments.
3. To make the wind vane pattern on the back of a paper plate
    a. Draw lines with a ruler and write wind directions as pictured on the file folder directions.
    b. Cut eight small slits around the edge of the plate (one at each wind direction line).
    c. Insert a brass fastener with string attached through the center of the plate.
4. *Optional:* You may want to make a pinwheel example following the directions on the student activity page.

DIRECTIONS FOR FILE FOLDER ACTIVITIES

Activity 1

The student makes a wind vane, referring to the teacher-made pattern.

Activity 2

The student makes the pinwheel using a copy of the student activity page labeled "pinwheel."

1. The student cuts out the square.
2. He or she carefully cuts the lines indicated on the square (starting at the corner, cutting toward the center).
3. The student pokes a straight pin through each of the corner dots on the square, then pokes the pin through the center dot and inserts the pin into the eraser of the pencil.

Follow-up activities

1. Pinwheel experiment: the student observes the movement of the pinwheel when he or she stands, walks, and runs with it outdoors.
2. Wind vane experiment: the student
    a. Lays the compass on a flat surface.
    b. Holds the wind vane in a horizontal position above the compass.
    c. Matches the wind vane directions with the compass directions.
    d. Determines the wind direction by watching the movement of the string.
    e. Places the string in the slit on the wind vane that corresponds with the direction of the wind.

Older students may record wind direction and estimate its speed by using a copy of the Beaufort Wind Scale. This scale can be found in books about weather forecasting such as Kaufmann, John, *Winds on Weather,* William Morrow and Co., New York, 1971; Sattler, Helen R., *Nature's Weather Forecasts,* Thomas Nelson, Inc., New York, 1978.

Wind

$\boxed{1}$ Make a wind vane. Use a compass with it.

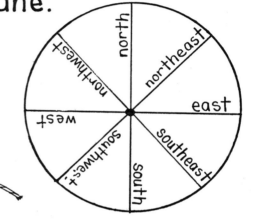

$\boxed{2}$ Make a pinwheel.

File Folder Directions

Pinwheel

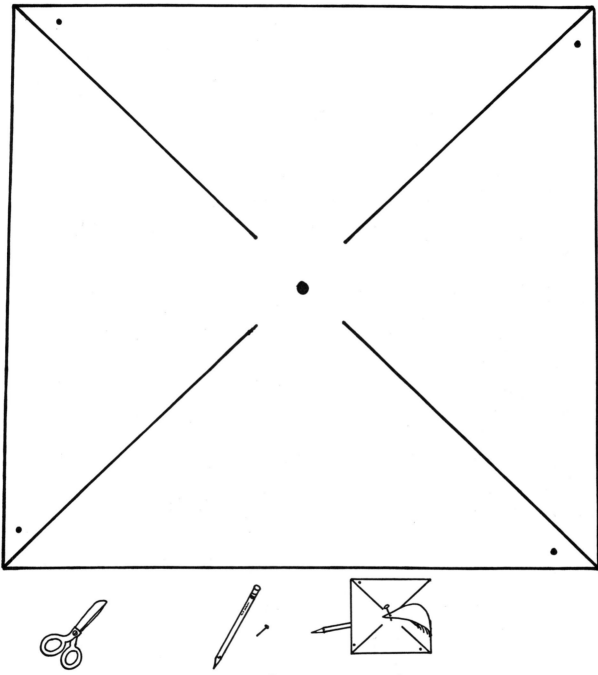

1. Cut on the lines.   2. Pin the •s to the eraser.

Student Activity Page

TEACHER'S DIRECTIONS FOR THE SNOW ACTIVITY

Content areas: Handwriting, teacher's choice (refer to page **x**)

Skills: Fine-motor coordination, teacher's choice, using reference materials

Materials needed:

> Copies of student activity pages
> One white bag 5½-by-10½ inches per student
> Crayons
> Pencil
> Scissors
> Glue
> References

Materials preparation:

1. Determine a skill to reinforce or review, such as spelling words, reading vocabulary, or snow-related words (blizzard, snowball, snowdrift, slush, snowflakes, slippery, snow, stormy, frigid, cold, and so on).
2. Make a reference list of the words or place appropriate references at this area.

DIRECTIONS FOR FILE FOLDER ACTIVITIES

Activity 1

> The student writes his or her name on the picture from the Blizzard Bag student activity page in this unit, then colors it, cuts it out, and pastes it on the bag.

Activity 2

> The student uses references to write the words on the snowballs on the student activity pages. He or she cuts out the snowballs and puts them in the bag.

Snow

1 Make a bag.

2 Put your words on the snow balls. Cut them out.

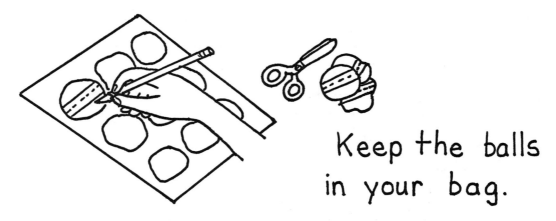

Keep the balls in your bag.

File Folder Directions

Blizzard Bag

This bag should be used on or before the next blizzard.

name

Student Activity Page

Copy your words onto the snowballs.

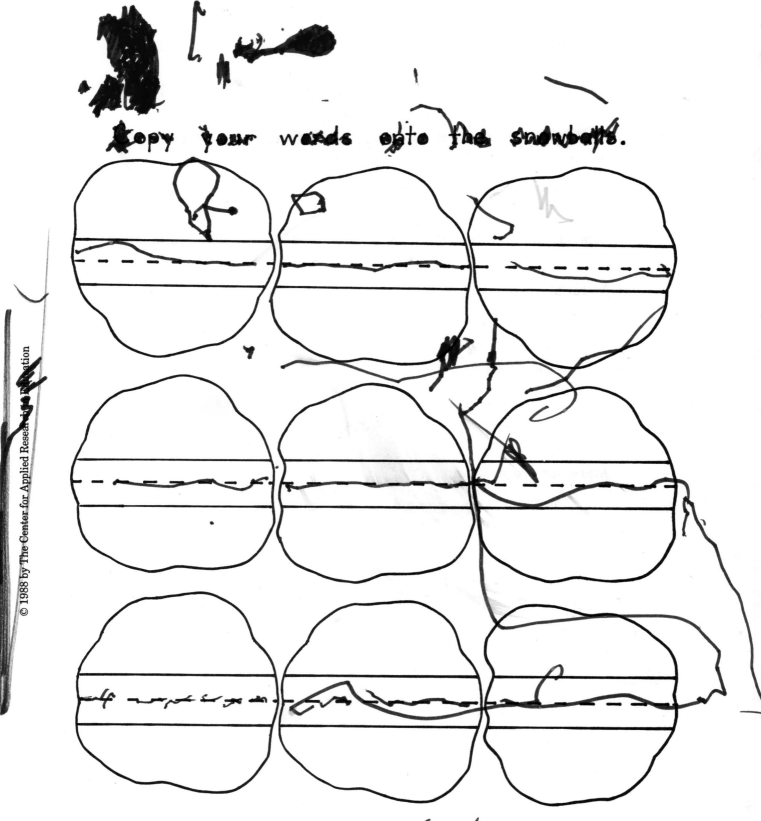

Student Activity Page

TEACHER'S DIRECTIONS FOR THE RAIN ACTIVITY

Content areas: Science, handwriting

Skills: Communication, observing, experimenting, fine-motor coordination

Materials needed:

Copies of student activity page	Ice cubes
Glass	Bowls
Plastic bag	Pencil
Paper towels	Crayons
Optional: tape recorder and cassette tape	

Materials preparation:

1. Establish background information about the water cycle using weather books such as Brandt, Keith, *What Makes It Rain?*, Troll Associates, Mahwah, N.J., 1982.
2. You may want to prepare a cassette tape of directions for the experiments at this center.

DIRECTIONS FOR FILE FOLDER ACTIVITIES

Activity 1

The student conducts the following experiments:

1. Rain (precipitation occurs when the temperature of water vapor chills. This causes condensation of the water vapor into droplets of rain or precipitation).

    a. Place ice cubes in a glass of cold water.
    b. Set the glass into a bowl of warm water.
    c. Observe the drops of water that form on the outside of the glass.

2. Evaporation (when water becomes warm enough it will become water vapor).

    a. Put two paper towels in a bowl of water, then squeeze the towels to remove excess water.
    b. Place one towel inside a plastic bag.
    c. Spread the other towel on the table.
    d. Observe that the towel on the table becomes dry, the towel in the bag remains wet.

Activity 2

The student colors the picture of the water cycle on the following student activity page. He or she completes the sentences on the student activity page.

Rain

1 Do experiments.

Put ice in a glass.

Put in warm water.
What happened?

Wet two towels.

Put one in a warm place.

Wait.
What will happen?

Put one in a bag.

2 Do the ditto.

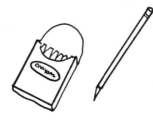 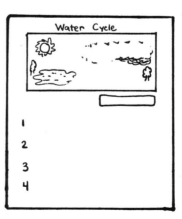

File Folder Directions

Water Cycle

2. Clouds fill with water vapor.

1. Water evaporates.

3. It rains.

Fill in the blank.

evaporated	cold
warm	rain

1. When water vapor cools it will _____.

2. The water in the warm towel _____.

3. When water vapor becomes _____ it can rain.

4. When water becomes _____ it will evaporate.

name _____

Student Activity Page

TEACHER'S DIRECTIONS FOR THE CLOUDS ACTIVITY

Content areas: Reading, art, science

Skills: Listening, creating, fine-motor coordination, classifying

Materials needed:

A medium for fingerpainting: shaving cream, soap flakes, or fingerpaint
Fingerpaint container
Blue paper to cover a tabletop
Clear plastic bag or clear Con-Tact paper
Masking tape
Old shirt
Tape recorder
Cassette tape
Pencil
Copies of student activity page
A book about clouds such as de Paola, Tomie, *The Cloud Book,* Scholastic Book Services, New York, 1975 or May, Julian, *The Clouds Book,* Creative Educational Society, Inc., Mankato, Minn., 1972

Materials preparation:

1. Prepare a cassette tape of the book.
2. Prepare a table for fingerpainting by
   a. Covering a table with blue paper.
   b. Taping a piece of clear plastic or clear Con-Tact paper over the blue paper.
   c. Setting a container of fingerpaint on the table.
3. Some fingerpaint medium ideas are
   a. Shaving cream from an aerosol container (caution students not to put it on their face and to avoid any mouth and eye contact)
   b. White fingerpaint
   c. Soap flakes and water: mix one-half cup of soap flakes, two tablespoons liquid laundry starch, and water until very thick

DIRECTIONS FOR FILE FOLDER ACTIVITIES

Activity 1

The student listens to the cassette tape of the book.

Activity 2

The student identifies the clouds in the pictures on the student activity page. He or she writes the names of the clouds under the pictures.

Activity 3

The student

1. Puts on the shirt.
2. Fingerpaints the four kinds of clouds pictured on the student activity page using a small amount of the medium.
3. Removes the fingerpaint from the table top and returns it to the container.
4. Cleans up the area and himself or herself.

 **Clouds**

1 Listen to the book.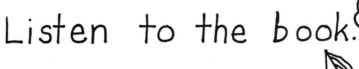

2 Do ditto.

3 Fingerpaint clouds.

© 1988 by The Center for Applied Research in Education

Clouds

cirrus   stratus
cumulus   nimbus

Write the name of the cloud under its picture.

TEACHER'S DIRECTIONS FOR THE LIGHTNING ACTIVITY

Content areas: Science, art

Skills: Creating, fine-motor coordination, experimenting, measuring, predicting

Materials needed:

Copies of student activity page (ditto on yellow construction paper)
Rubber comb
Nail
Bobby pin
Ruler
Cotton balls
Glue
Pencil

Hammer
Scissors
Piece of wool fabric, approximately 6-by-6 inches
Small pieces of paper
One 5-foot piece of orange yarn per student
One aluminum foil pie pan per student
One 12-inch pipe cleaner per student
Paper puncher

Materials preparation: You may want to use weather books and audiovisual aids to establish background about lightning, static electricity, and thunder.

DIRECTIONS FOR FILE FOLDER ACTIVITIES

Activity 1

The student rubs a rubber comb on a piece of wool then holds it over pieces of paper. (The paper will jump to meet the comb, demonstrating static electricity.)

Activity 2

The student uses the following instructions to make a lightning mobile:

1. Cut out the lightning shapes on the student activity page.
2. Use a paper puncher to punch holes on each "x" in the lightning shapes.
3. Measure and cut the yarn into five 12-inch pieces.
4. Tie a knot at one end of a piece of yarn. Thread the opposite end of the yarn through a bobby pin and "sew" the lightning shape. Do this for each lightning shape.
5. Use a paper puncher to make five holes around the edge of the pie pan.
6. Tie the lightning shapes to the holes on the pie pan.
7. Make a hole in the center of the pie-pan with a hammer and a nail.
8. Put a pipe cleaner through the hole and tie a knot in it to form a hanger.
9. Glue cotton balls to form a cloud on the pie pan.

Lightning

1 Do experiment.

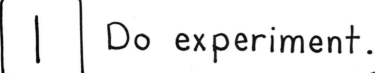

wool

Rub comb.

← paper

What happened?

2 Make a lightning mobile.

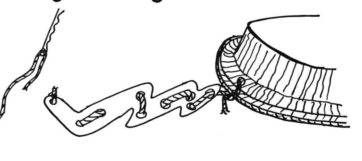

Cut out lightning.

Punch holes.

Sew yarn in the holes.
Tie to your plate.

Glue on a cotton "cloud."

File Folder Directions

Lightning

Student Activity Page

TEACHER'S DIRECTIONS FOR THE RAINBOWS ACTIVITY

Content areas: Science, art

Skills: Creating, experimenting, observing

Materials needed:

Prism	Easel
Pan of water	Red, orange, yellow, green, blue,
Mirror	indigo, and violet paint (place in
Paint paper	this order on the easel)

Materials preparation:

1. Set up this activity near a window.
2. Discuss rainbows and the spectrum.

DIRECTIONS FOR FILE FOLDER ACTIVITIES

Activity 1

The student conducts the following two rainbow experiments:

1. Prism: The student holds a prism in a path of sunlight to observe the colors of the rainbow.
2. Mirror:
   a. The student puts a mirror in a pan of water where the sun can shine directly on it. (Lean the mirror against the side of the pan under the water.)
   b. The student moves the mirror slightly until he or she observes a row of rainbow colors on the ceiling or wall.

Activity 2

The student paints a rainbow using the paint in the order placed on the easel.

Rainbows

1 Make a rainbow 2 ways.

← mirror

← water

↗ prism

2 Paint a rainbow.

Use these colors:

red
orange
yellow
green
blue
indigo
violet

File Folder Directions

TEACHER'S DIRECTIONS FOR THE SEASONS ACTIVITY

Content areas: Handwriting, art, science

Skills: Creating, communication, fine-motor coordination, creative writing

Materials needed:

Copies of student activity page
9-by-12-inch newsprint
Crayons
Pencil
Stapler and staples

Materials preparation:

You may need to establish background information about seasons using a good book such as Branley, Franklyn, *Sunshine Makes the Seasons,* Thomas Y. Crowell Co., New York, 1974.

1. A younger student may make a four page book illustrating the seasons (in addition to the cover, which is a copy of the student activity page "Seasons of the Earth." He or she may write a different season on each page and illustrate it, for instance, showing the appropriate changes in weather, trees, and people's clothing. You may want to make an example book with the seasons written in it for the student to copy. An older student may have a book several pages long. He or she may write a few sentences about each season and illustrate them.

2. You might prefer to staple the younger students' books together for them before they begin. Older students might staple their books together after completing the pages.

DIRECTIONS FOR FILE FOLDER ACTIVITIES

Activity 1

The student colors the student activity page cover.

Activity 2

The student writes, illustrates, and assembles his or her book according to your book directions.

Seasons

1 Color the cover.

2 Do the pages.

File Folder Directions

Seasons of the Earth

spring

summer

winter

fall

This book
belongs to

_____

Student Activity Page

Weather
Enrichment Activities

TEACHER'S SUGGESTIONS FOR WEATHER ENRICHMENT ACTIVITIES

1. Weather Group Activities (refer to pp. 41–43)

Balloon Launch

2. Weather Home Study (refer to p. 44)

Encourage students to record weather data on their calendars.

3. Weather Award (refer to p. 45)

Ditto the page on colored paper. Give each student who returns the Home Study calendar a Home Study Award. The Weather Award may be used for the recognition of good work and so on.

4. Weather Evaluation (refer to p. 46)

The evaluations may be stapled to the student's weather related work. The grade may be based on a joint teacher-student decision. The student colors the thermometer with a red crayon to indicate the degree of his or her performance level. The student may also write numerals on the lines of the thermometer.

5. Weather Balloon (refer to p. 47)

This page may be used for an experience story following the "Balloon Launch" group activity or for creative writing. Some ideas are "If I rode in my balloon . . . " "What if my balloon landed in . . . "

6. Weather Rainbow (refer to p. 48)

The student writes in the missing letters, completes the crossword puzzle, and colors the rainbow.

7. Weather Vocabulary (Kite) (refer to p. 49)

Ditto the page on construction paper. Write nine adjectives on the chalkboard describing wind (breezy, blustery, howling, chilly, and so on). The student copies the words in the nine rectangles at the bottom of the page. He or she makes a kite out of the square at the top of the page and attaches a yarn tail. He or she cuts-out and pastes the word strips onto nine construction paper strips on the tail. Then he or she writes a story about the wind on the kite using some of the words. You may want to write poems for an optional activity.

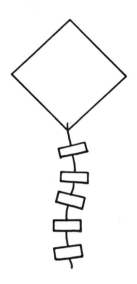

8. Weather Journal (refer to p. 50)

Make an eight-page weather journal for the students to write in and illustrate daily. The student records the dates and weather at the top of each page. He or she might write about the clothes worn to school, recess activity, home activity, and so on.

GROUP ACTIVITIES

As a group activity to culminate the weather unit launch helium-filled balloons. Students may want to give this project a name, such as "Operation _____" or "Project _____."

In a preparation for the balloon launch, you will need to

1. Recruit parent help (by sending the preceding parent letter, refer to page 4) to type postcards, blow up the balloons, tie on strings, help students attach information bags onto balloons, and so on.

2. Arrange to rent a tank of helium. Consult "Rental Equipment" in the Yellow Pages of your telephone directory.

3. Purchase string and balloons (buy at least 10 more balloons than the number of students to allow for breakage).

4. Purchase for each student a plastic sandwich bag, an index card, and a postcard.

5. Plan a writing lesson prior to the balloon launch in which the student writes the following information on an index card. You might use a ditto form or typed card for younger students.

> "I am a student at _____.
>   *name of school*
> As a weather activity, I launched this balloon on _____
> _____.
>
> Please return the postcard to me. Thank you."
>
> _____
>   *student's name*

6. Have students write or parents type the following information on postcards. Put the school address on one side and this information on the other side:

> Dear _____
>   *student's name*
> I found your balloon on _____
> at _____.
>   *location*
>
> _____
>   *finder's signature*

7. Have each student put an index card and a stamped postcard in the plastic bag and tie it onto his or her balloon on the day of the launch.

Follow-up Activities

1. Center group discussions on predictions about how high the balloons will travel, where the balloons will travel, where the balloons will land, when the first postcard will be received, whose card will it be, and so on.
2. Correspond with persons who return the postcards.
3. Place pins in a map at the locations where the balloons were found.
4. Enrichment page (refer to p. 47) may be used for an experience story or creative writing.

Optional Group Activities

1. You may want to conduct weather experiments.
2. You may want to have students make weather vanes, rain gauges, wind anemometers, and barometers to use at a class weather station. The following books might be helpful in preparing these instruments: Trowbridge, Leslie W., *Experiments in Meteorology,* Doubleday and Co., Inc., Garden City, New York, 1973; Yerian, Cameron, *Fun Time Projects: Earth and Sky,* Children's Press, Chicago, 1974.

**Weather Home Study
Enrichment Page**

Return by _____

Date _____

Dear Parent,

We will begin a Science Weather Unit this week. Please have your child record data on the weather calendar from _____

date

to _____.

date

He or she will need to record daily the date, temperature at _____,

time

and an appropriate weather symbol such as sun, rain, cloudy, snow, and so on. The calendar data will be compared and shared with the class on _____.

date

Thank you very much for your continued support.

Sincerely,

_____

Your child's teacher

Child's name _____

Parent signature _____

Sunday	Monday	Tuesday	Wednesday	Thursday	Friday	Saturday

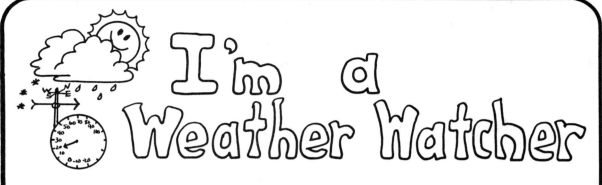

I'm a Weather Watcher

I recorded the weather
for two weeks.

_____
name

Home Study Award

Cloudy, Sunny,
Wet or Dry.
Sure do like
The way you try !

_____
_____

Weather Award

name _____

date _____

I am learning about weather.

My _____ work was:

name _____

date _____

I am learning about weather.
Today I worked on the
_____ activity.

My work was:

Weather Evaluation Page

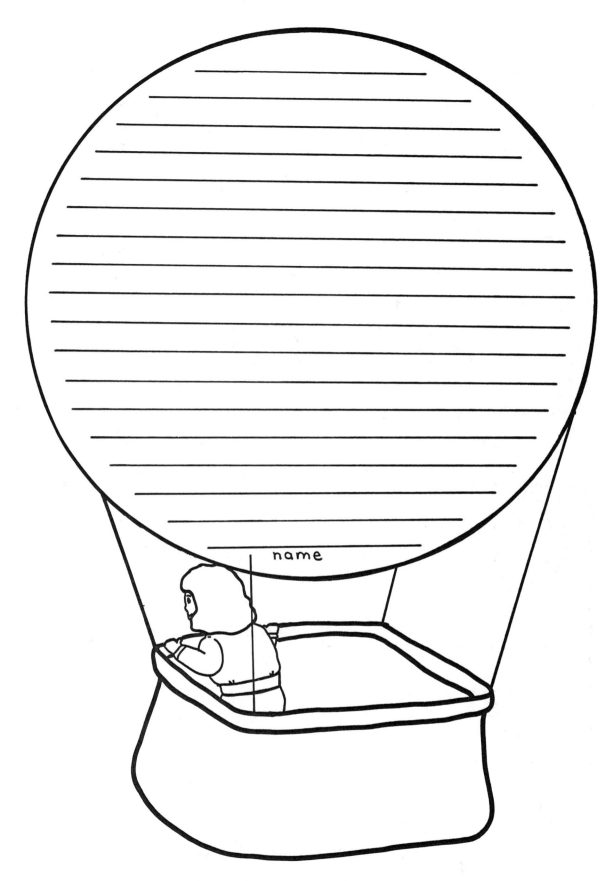

name

Weather: Balloon Enrichment Page

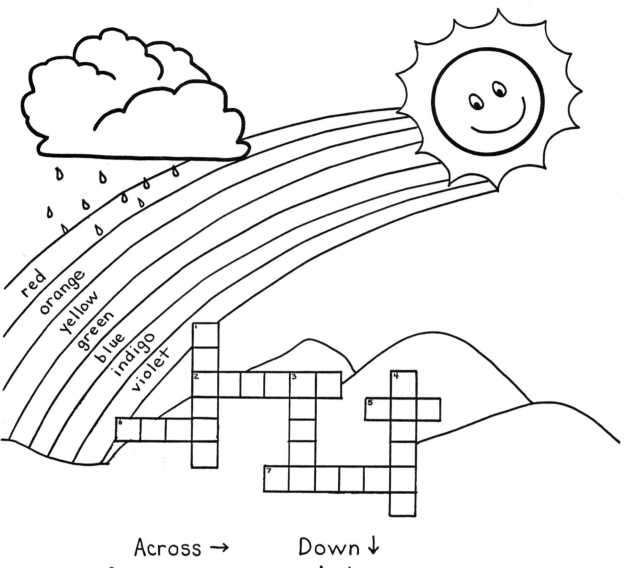

red orange yellow green blue indigo violet

Across →
2. o_a_ge
5. _ ed
6. b_u_
7. i_dig_

Down ↓
1. vi_le_
3. _re_n
4. ye_lo_

name _____

Weather: Rainbow Enrichment Page

Weather: Kite Enrichment Page

Today:
the weather is

Today I

Yesterday:
the weather was

Yesterday I

Weather: Journal Enrichment Page

© 1988 by The Center for Applied Research in Education

name

Unit 2
NUTRITION

NUTRITION NEWS

Date _____

Dear Parent,

Our next science unit will be about nutrition. Your child will learn about the four food groups: (1) grain, (2) fruits and vegetables, (3) milk, and (4) meat. He or she will learn about the daily serving suggestions.

As one of the art activities, your child will create place mats for your dinner table. Please encourage your child to set the table at home with these place mats.

Math activities will emphasize writing the numbers from _____ to _____ and counting money. You can help at home by reviewing the names and values of coins.

Your child will make a peanuts game. Please encourage him to play the game with you. You may want to discuss the products containing peanuts which you have at home.

As a group project we will make pan pizzas on _____ for lunch in our room. The pizza will contain something from each of the four food groups. Please note the date if you would be willing to help. I will send another letter prior to this project for definite arrangements.

Thank you for your continued support.

Sincerely,

_____
Your child's teacher

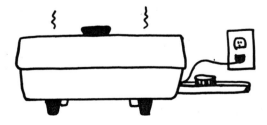

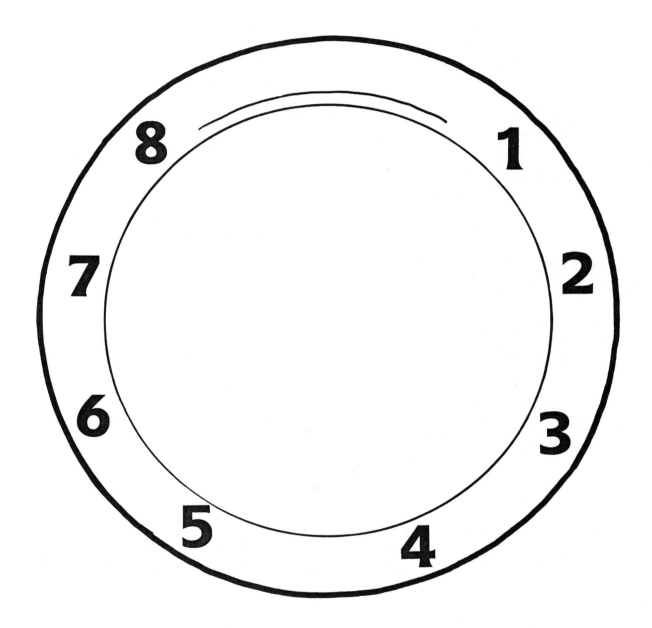

Nutrition Center Marker

NUTRITION CENTER MARKER

A learning center marker is provided for students using the science unit activities at learning centers (refer to p. 246).

Distribute copies of the preceding plate marker to the students. The students can draw food on their markers, cut out their markers, and place them near the Nutrition Learning Centers.

NUTRITION ACTIVITIES LIST

These activities relate to various aspects of nutrition, with emphasis on the four basic food groups.

1. Four Food Groups Activity (A bulletin board is used with this activity)

Content areas: Science, reading

Skills: Sorting, classifying, fine-motor coordination

Activities:

a. Tack food pictures onto the four food group areas on the bulletin board.
b. Write food names or draw food pictures on the student activity page.

2. Yummy Fruits Activity

Content areas: Spelling, reading, handwriting

Skills: Fine-motor coordination, alphabetical order, matching, using reference materials

Activities:

a. Use magnetic letters to spell fruit names.
b. Trace and write fruit names on student activity page.
c. *Optional:* Cut out and arrange fruit pictures in alphabetical order in a book.

3. Peanuts Activity (Open-ended activity)

Content areas: Science and teacher's choice, handwriting

Skills: Observing, matching, fine-motor coordination, teacher's choice, experimenting, using reference materials, classifying

Activities:

a. Shell and rub a peanut on brown kraft paper to extract oil.

b. Play a teacher-made peanut game.

c. Make your own peanut game.

4. Set the Table Activity

Content areas: Art, science

Skills: Creating, sorting, fine-motor coordination

Activities:

a. Carve design in a piece of potato.

b. Make potato print place mats for family members.

c. Set the table.

5. I Like to Eat Activity

Content areas: Reading, handwriting

Skills: Listening, creative writing, communicating, fine-motor coordination, using reference materials, creating

Activities:

a. Listen to story about tasting.

b. Make an "I Like to Eat" book.

6. The Food Store Activity

Content areas: Math, science

Skills: Ordering, sorting, matching, fine-motor coordination, using reference materials

Activities:

a. Arrange food products from lowest to highest prices.

b. Match money cards to food products.

c. Record products and prices on paper.

d. Trace coins to show corresponding values.

7. Milk the Cow Activity

Content areas: Math, handwriting, science

Skills: Ordering, sorting, measuring time, fine-motor coordination, using reference materials

Activities:

a. Race the sand timer to order the numbers on the gameboard.
b. Write the numbers on the student activity page.

8. Food Sorting Activity

Content area: Art

Skills: Sorting, creating, fine-motor coordination, ordering, matching

Activities:

a. Sort foods into a muffin pan.
b. Design a food picture on a paper plate by punching holes and sewing it.

TEACHER'S DIRECTIONS FOR THE FOUR FOOD GROUPS ACTIVITY

Content areas: Science, reading

Skills: Sorting, classifying, fine-motor coordination

Materials needed:

> Copies of the student activity page
> Teacher-made food picture-word cards and container
> Pins or thumbtacks and container
> Bulletin board
> Crayons
> Pencil

Materials preparation:

1. Prepare the "4 for Your Body" bulletin board as shown here.

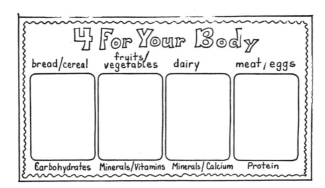

2. Make four or five food picture-word cards for each of the four food groups (refer to "The 4 Food Groups" file folder directions. Write the names of the foods under the picture on each card. (Laminate the cards or cover them with clear Con-Tact paper.)
3. Provide a container for the cards.

DIRECTIONS FOR FILE FOLDER ACTIVITIES

Activity 1

The student tacks each food card to the correct food group area on the bulletin board. He or she may refer to the "4 Food Groups" on the file folder directions page.

Activity 2

1. The student copies the food names from the bulletin board in the correct squares of the shopping bag on the student activity page. A younger student may draw pictures.
2. The student takes the food cards off the bulletin board and returns them to the container.

The 4 Food Groups

1 Pin the cards to the right boxes.

bread/cereal

muffin

tacks

cards

2 Do ditto.

The 4 Food Groups

name _____

File Folder Directions

bread / cereal

fruit / vegetable

The
4
Food Groups

dairy

meat/eggs

File Folder Directions

The 4 Food Groups

bread / cereal

fruit / vegetable

dairy

meat / eggs

Name _____

Student Activity Page

TEACHER'S DIRECTIONS FOR THE YUMMY FRUITS ACTIVITY

Content areas: Spelling, reading, handwriting

Skills: Fine-motor coordination, alphabetical order, matching, using reference materials

Materials needed:

> Copies of student activity page
> Set of twenty-six lowercase magnetic letters
> Six fruit-shaped magnets or six teacher-made fruit cards
> Metallic chalkboard or portable metal board
> Pencil
> Crayons

Materials preparation:

If fruit magnets are unavailable, make six 6 by 6 inch fruit picture cards of the fruits shown on the student activity page. Attach the cards to the chalkboard, leaving space under the cards for the student to spell the words with magnetic letters.

DIRECTIONS FOR FILE FOLDER ACTIVITIES

Activity 1

The student uses the magnetic letters to spell the name of each fruit on the board (common letters will need to be shared unless a very large set is used). The student may refer to the student activity page for the correct spelling of the fruits.

Activity 2

The student traces then writes the name of each fruit on the student activity page.

Optional activity

An older student might cut apart the six fruit pictures on the student activity page and arrange them in alphabetical order. The pictures could then be stapled into a book.

Yummy Fruits

1 Spell the fruits with letters.

apple

2 Do ditto.

File Folder Directions

Yummy Fruits

Trace.

Write.

apple   pear   orange

bananas   grapes   peach

Fruits have vitamins that keep us healthy.
Fruits give us energy. _____
I like to eat _____
_____
name _____

Student Activity Page

TEACHER'S DIRECTIONS FOR THE PEANUTS ACTIVITY

Content areas: Science, teacher's choice (refer to page **x**), handwriting

Skills: Observing, matching, experimenting, fine-motor coordination, teacher's choice, using reference materials, classifying

Materials needed:

> Copies of student activity page (ditto on heavy paper)
> One unshelled peanut per student
> Container for peanuts
> One 4-by-4-inch piece of kraft paper per student
> One small brown bag or envelope per student
> Pencil
> Scissors
> Teacher-made peanuts matching game
> Teacher-made reference chart

Materials preparation:

1. To make the peanuts matching game use a copy of the Peanuts student activity page to reinforce or review a skill. Some ideas are: upper and lowercase letters, color words and colors, number words and numerals, contractions, and opposite words. Write the words or numerals on the peanuts and cut them out. Then cut each peanut apart differently to make the game self-checking.
2. Laminate the game and provide a container for it.
3. Make a reference chart by writing words and numerals on a copy of the student activity page.
4. Be sure your students have background information about peanuts and products containing peanut oil. You may wish to refer to the following book: Selsam, Millicent E., *Peanut,* William Morrow and Co., New York, 1969.

DIRECTIONS FOR FILE FOLDER ACTIVITIES

Activity 1

1. The student shells one peanut, rubs it on a piece of brown kraft paper, and observes the spot of peanut oil.
2. The student may eat the peanut.

Activity 2

The student plays the teacher-made peanuts game.

Activity 3

The student makes a peanut game of his or her own, referring to yours occasionally. He or she then puts the game in a bag.

Optional activity

The student may circle the pictures of edible things on the file folder directions page with a water-based marking pen.

Peanuts

1 Shell one peanut.
Rub it on brown paper.
What can you see?
You may eat the peanut.

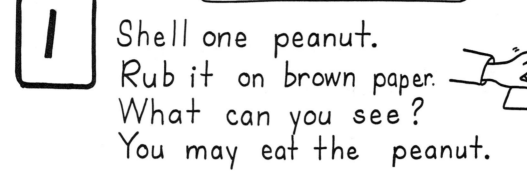

2 Match the peanuts game.

3 Make your game.

Write.

Cut it out.

File Folder Directions

Here are 8 things made from peanuts. Some are made from peanut oil. Which can we eat?

SOAP

COOKIES

Shaving Cream

Cooking Oil

PAINT

Margarine

Plastic toys

Candy

File Folder Directions

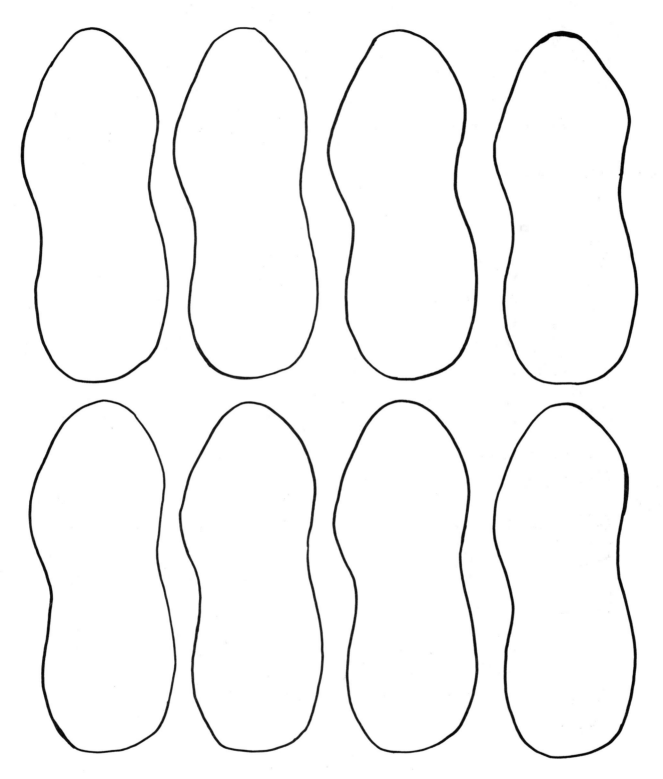

Student Activity Page

TEACHER'S DIRECTIONS FOR THE SET THE TABLE ACTIVITY

Content areas: Art, science

Skills: Creating, sorting, fine-motor coordination

Materials needed:

> Teacher-made place mat
> Enough potatoes for half the number of students
> Container and lid for potatoes
> Easel
> Old shirt
> Tempera paint
> Container and lid for paint
> Sponge (piece to fit bottom of paint container)
> Enough 12-by-18-inch heavy paper for each student and his or her family members
> Five of each of the following table setting items: napkins, plates, cups, knives, spoons, forks, and place mats.

Materials preparation:

1. To make a place mat, glue, tape, or staple one of each of the table setting items (paper and plastic) on a place mat. The example will show the proper way to set table service.
2. Each day cut two potatoes in half and put them in a container. Students may wash off the potatoes and return them to the container when they are finished. At the end of the day, discard the potatoes and rinse the container.

DIRECTIONS FOR FILE FOLDER ACTIVITIES

Activity 1

1. The student clips the paper to the easel.
2. The student uses the table knife, under adult supervision, to carve a potato. (You may need to cut potatoes for younger students.)
3. The student dips the potato into the sponge of tempera paint and prints a border around the place mat. He or she continues in this way to make place mats for each family member.
4. The student cleans up the learning center while the place mats are drying.

Activity 2

The student sets the table with the table service, referring to your place mat.

Set the Table

1 Carve a potato half.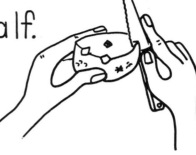

2 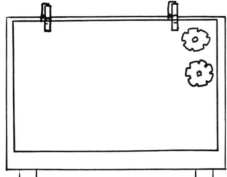 Make borders on place mats.

 Make a place mat for each person in your family.

3 Set the table at the center.

File Folder Directions

© 1988 by The Center for Applied Research in Education

TEACHER'S DIRECTIONS FOR THE I LIKE TO EAT ACTIVITY

Content areas: Reading, handwriting

Skills: Listening, creative writing, communicating, using reference materials, fine motor coordination, creating

Materials needed:

> Copies of student activity pages
> Pencil
> Crayons
> Pictionary or dictionary
> Tape recorder
> Cassette tape
> A book about tasting (likes and dislikes) such as Fisher, Aileen, *No Accounting for Tastes,* Bowmar, Glendale, CA, 1973

Materials preparation:

1. Tape record the book you have chosen for this center.
2. Encourage students to think of foods they like and don't like.

DIRECTIONS FOR FILE FOLDER ACTIVITIES

Activity 1

The student listens to the story.

Activity 2

1. The student uses the student activity page to draw on the plate the food he or she likes. (An older student may write an "I Like to Eat" story on the back of the page using the pictionary or dictionary as a reference.)
2. The student uses the student activity page to draw on the plate the food he or she does not like to eat. (An older student may write an "I Don't Like to Eat" story on the back of the page.)

Follow-up activity

The students' stories may be compiled in a class book.

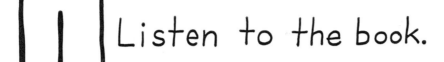

I Like to Eat...

1 Listen to the book.

2 Make the book.

File Folder Directions

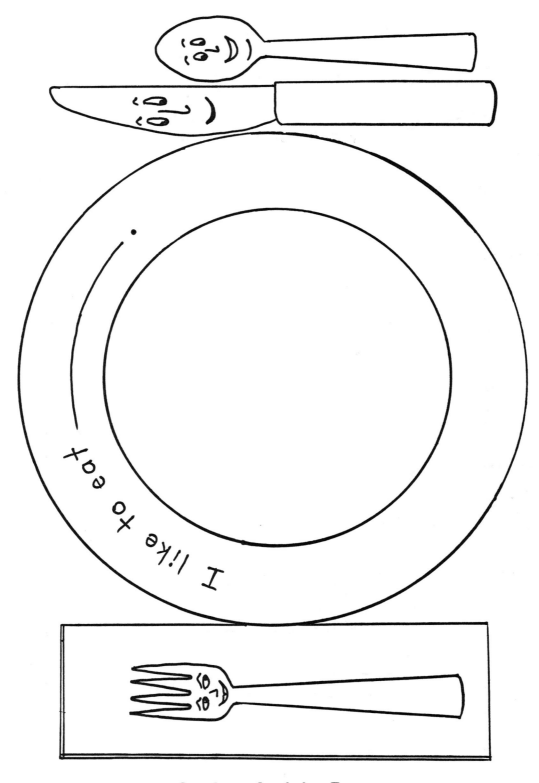

I like to eat

Student Activity Page

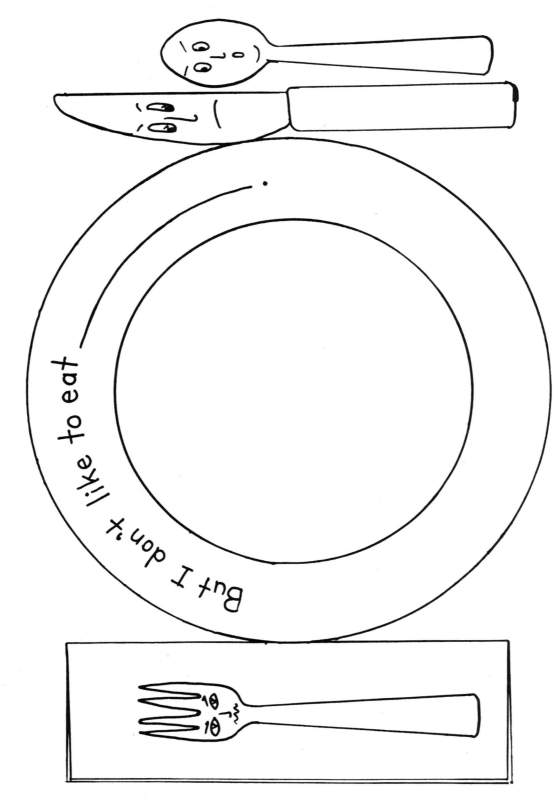

I like to eat _____

But I don't like to eat _____

Student Activity Page

TEACHER'S DIRECTIONS FOR THE FOOD STORE ACTIVITY

Content areas: Math, science

Skills: Ordering, sorting, matching, fine-motor coordination, using reference materials

Materials needed:

> Teacher-made grocery game
> Toy cash register or envelope
> 12-by-18-inch paper
> Pencil
> Crayons
> Container of real or play coins
> Reference chart

Materials preparation:

1. To make the grocery game you need:
    > Eight empty food containers (boxes, cans, and so on)
    > Grocery bag or box for the containers
    > Eight 3-by-5-inch index cards
    > Money ink stamps or realistic play coins
    > Eight pieces of paper for price tags

    a. Write the price of the eight foods on tags placed on the top of each container. The prices will vary according to your students' ability, and they will be different for each container.
    b. Stamp or glue coins equal to the prices on the index cards. (The correct amount of money may be written on the back of the card to make each one self-checking.)
    c. The cards should be kept in an envelope or cash register.

2. Make a chart of coins and their values appropriate for the game, such as 1¢ = penny.

DIRECTIONS FOR FILE FOLDER ACTIVITIES:

Activity 1

The student sorts the food containers and arranges them on the floor in order of least expensive price to most expensive price.

Activity 2

The student matches the money cards to the corresponding price tag on each food container.

Activity 3

The student folds a paper into an eight-box format. He or she copies the price tags from least expensive to most expensive, then draws the appropriate foods. The student traces the coins that will equal the cost of each food under the pictures.

The Food Store

1 Arrange the food from the lowest to highest price.

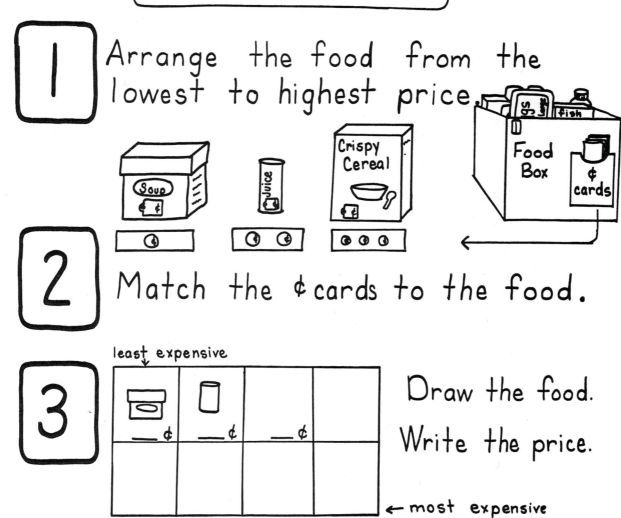

2 Match the ¢ cards to the food.

3 Draw the food. Write the price.

least expensive ↓

__ ¢   __ ¢   __ ¢

← most expensive

Now trace around the coins to show the prices.

__ ¢

4 coins

File Folder Directions

TEACHER'S DIRECTIONS FOR THE MILK THE COW ACTIVITY

Content areas: Math, handwriting, science

Skills: Ordering, sorting, measuring time, fine-motor coordination, using reference materials

Materials needed:

Copies of student activity page	Teacher-made game
Plastic milk jug or container	Reference chart
50 milk jug caps or poker chips	Pencil
Black permanent marking pen	Crayons
One-minute hourglass	

Materials preparation:

1. To make the game, you need:
    12-by-18-inch file folder or posterboard
    50 self-sticking dots (40 of color A, 5 of color B, 5 of color C)
    50 milk jug caps (40 of color A, 5 of color B, 5 of color C)

    a. Determine the skill you want to reinforce or review. Some ideas are counting from 1 to 50, counting from 50 to 100, counting by fives to 250, and counting Roman numerals I to L.
    b. Lay the dots on the file folder as shown in the illustration.

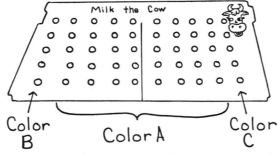

    c. Write numbers on the milk jug caps with a permanent black marking pen. Use B caps for the beginning numbers in each row. The color A caps are used for the eight middle numbers in each row. (The different colors aid the student in sorting the caps in order.)
    d. You may want to make a container for the caps by cutting a plastic milk jug as shown in the file folder directions.

2. Make a reference chart by writing the numbers on a copy of the student activity page.

DIRECTIONS FOR FILE FOLDER ACTIVITIES

Activity 1

The student turns the hourglass upside down. He or she then tries to place the milk caps in order on the gameboard before the hourglass runs out. The student may use the reference chart.

Activity 2

The student writes the numbers on the student activity page.

Milk the Cow

1 Play the game.

2 Write the numbers.

File Folder Directions

Milk the Cow

name _____

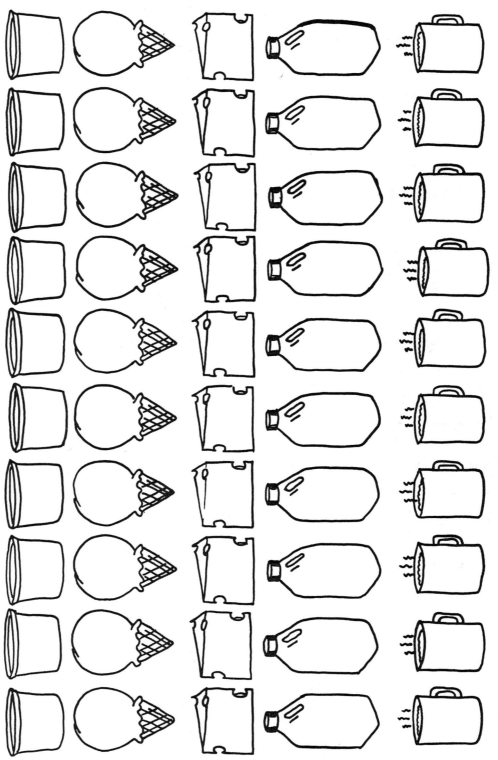

Student Activity Page

TEACHER'S DIRECTIONS FOR THE FOOD SORTING ACTIVITY

Content area: Art

Skills: Sorting, creating, fine-motor coordination, matching, ordering

Materials needed:

Six-cup muffin tin	Bobby pin
One small paper plate per student	Glue
One 3-foot piece of yarn per student	Pencil
Scissors	Paper puncher

Container with six types of dry food (for example, corn, beans, seeds, cereal, and macaroni products of different shapes and sizes).

DIRECTIONS FOR FILE FOLDER ACTIVITIES

Activity 1

The student will sort all of the foods into the muffin tin.

Activity 2

1. The student punches holes around edge of a small paper plate with a paper puncher.
2. He or she ties one end of a piece of yarn through a hole in the plate. (You may want to punch the first hole and tie yarn through it for younger students.)
3. Thread the opposite end of the yarn through a bobby pin. Use the bobby pin as a needle to sew yarn around the edge of the plate. Tie the two ends of the yarn into a bow.
4. Glue food onto the middle of the plate in a pattern or free-form design.

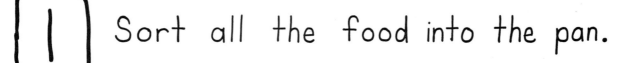

Food Sorting

1 Sort all the food into the pan.

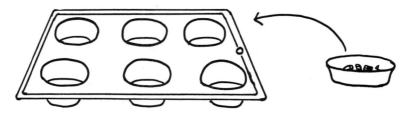

2 Make a picture with some of the food on a plate.

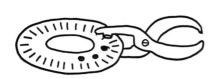

1. Make holes.

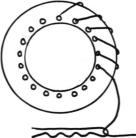

2. String yarn.   3. Make a bow.

4. Glue on the food in middle.

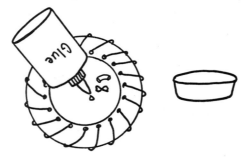

File Folder Directions

Nutrition
Enrichment Activities

TEACHER'S SUGGESTIONS FOR NUTRITION ENRICHMENT ACTIVITIES

1. **Nutrition Group Activities** (refer to pp. 88–90)

   Pizza Party

2. **Nutrition Home Study** (refer to p. 91)

   Encourage students to help plan their family's menus. Discuss the four food groups. Compare menus when they are returned.

3. **Nutrition Award** (refer to p. 93)

   Ditto the page on colored paper. Give each child who returns the Home Study Family Menu a Home Study Award. The Nutrition Award may be used for the recognition of good work and so on.

4. **Nutrition Evaluation** (refer to p. 94)

   The evaluations may be stapled to the student's nutrition related work. The grade may be based on a joint teacher-student decision. The student will write numerals on the scales such as 0, 20, 40, 60, 80, 100. He or she will draw an arrow from the dot at the base of the scale to the appropriate numeral to indicate his or her performance level.

5. **Nutrition Pizza** (refer to p. 95)

   This page may be used for an experience story following the group pan pizza activity (refer to p. 88) or for creative writing. You may wish to write key vocabulary words around the pizza outline prior to dittoing. Some ideas are: first, second, next, then, finally, taste, delicious, smell, chop, bake, roll, spread, meat, cheese, pepperoni, ham, sausage, dough, peppers, tomato, sauce, olives, onion, and so on.

6. **Nutrition Shopping** (refer to p. 96)

   Students may use newspapers, magazines, or coupons to cut out and paste "four food" advertisements including the price in each box on the shopping cart. Trace around real coins or make rubbings of coins to show the money value of each price.

7. Nutrition Vocabulary (Words About) (refer to p. 97)

Students may use a pictionary or dictionary to find eight words to write in each box on this page. Then they draw the appropriate picture above each word. Some ideas are: find eight vegetables, find eight fruits, list eight fruits in alphabetical order, find eight foods you would like to eat in one day, and so on.

GROUP ACTIVITIES

You may need to revise the letter to parents requesting pizza items (refer to p. 89) depending on the students' preferences.

Prior to sending the letter, a class discussion should be held to determine your students' choices of pizza ingredients. You may want to make a list of ingredients on the chalkboard. Encourage the students to think of the food groups for the ingredients (the food group number could be written next to each one). Remind the students that they will be allowed to remove any unwanted ingredients from their pieces of pizza.

On the day that you make pan pizzas, write the following steps on large chart paper: (1) wash hands, (2) grease pan and hands, (3) push dough to edges of pan, (4) spread the sauce, (5) sprinkle on cheese, (6) cut ingredients into small pieces, (7) sprinkle on mushrooms, meats, onions, and other additions, (8) cover with the lid, (9) wash hands, (10) bake, (11) eat. (You may want to have the students copy this chart for their boardwork activity.)

The group pan pizza activity can be handled in a quiet, efficient way with the help of two or three parents. During the morning the students will follow the regular morning schedule. The parents will work with one group of students during their seatwork or boardwork time (approximately half an hour) at a prearranged area while you work with reading groups.

One child may serve as a recorder in each group to list the ingredients in their pizza. The lists may be referred to by all of the students when they are ready to eat the pizzas.

One pan of pizza will yield approximately six servings. Larger groups may need to make two pizzas. As each pizza is made, cover it with the lid. After all of the groups have prepared the pizzas, bake them at the same time at 350 degrees for 20 to 30 minutes, then eat them. (CAUTION: Be sure this is done only under adult supervision.)

Follow-up Activities

1. Enrichment page may be used for an experience story or creative writing.
2. Parent thank-you notes may also be written.

PIZZA PARTY

Date _____

Dear Parent,

   Our pan pizza party will be on _____ at _____.
   The pizza will contain something from each of the four food groups. Your child will need to bring a piece of fruit, a vegetable, and _____ cents for milk to complete his or her lunch.
   On the following page is a list of ingredients the children have helped me prepare that is necessary for pan pizzas. Please decide which items you would be willing to contribute and return the list to me by _____. I will notify you which of the items you should send to school.
   We will be baking the pizzas in electric frying pans. If you are willing to share a frying pan with us, please indicate that on the list.
   We will need two to three parents to help make the pizzas. We will begin making pizzas at _____ and eat them by _____. If you would like to help, please indicate that on the list.
   Thank you for your continued support.

Sincerely,

_____
Your child's teacher

(Your child's name) _____

     I would be willing to send in any of the following items I have **checked for the Pan Pizza lunch:**

_____ paper plates _____
                no.

_____ paper napkins _____
                 no.

_____ 8-ounce package pizza cheese

_____ 6-ounce can pizza sauce

_____ onion

_____ sliced pepperoni

_____ ham

_____ cooked sausage (or smoky links)

_____ 1 loaf frozen bread dough

_____ small can mushrooms

_____ shortening (1 cup)

_____ I can send any *one* of the above ingredients.

_____ I can bring in my electric frying pan and lid on _____
                                                        day

_____ I will come to school by _____ on _____.
                             time   *day*
to help a small group of children make pan pizza. I will bring two sharp knives, 1 spatula, and 1 pancake turner.

Signed: _____   Phone: _____

Please return this note by _____.
I will contact you for definite arrangements.

**Nutrition Home Study
Enrichment Activity Page**
Return by _____

Home Study

Date _____

Dear Parent,

    Your child has been studying the four food groups in our Science Nutrition Unit.

    Please help your child plan your family's menus for one day. Include two servings from the meat group, four servings from the fruit-vegetable group, four servings from the grain group, and four servings from the milk group.

    You may extend this activity by taking your child on a shopping trip to buy the food. Through this experience, he or she will gain a better understanding of the task of planning and purchasing food.

    Please return the menus by _____.

Thank you for your continued support.

Sincerely,

_____
Your child's teacher

_____'s **Family Menus for** _____
                    child's name   *date*

Breakfast   **Lunch**   **Dinner**

_____   _____   _____

_____   _____   _____

_____   _____   _____

_____   _____   _____

_____   _____   _____

_____   _____   _____

_____   _____   _____

Snacks _____

I helped plan my
family's menus
for one day.

_____
my name

_____
Parent signature

Comments: Please write on the back of this page.

I helped plan my family's menus for one day.

_____
my name

Home Study Award

Just wanted you to know...

_____

_____

_____

_____

Nutrition Award

name _____

date _____

I am learning about Nutrition.

My _____ work was:

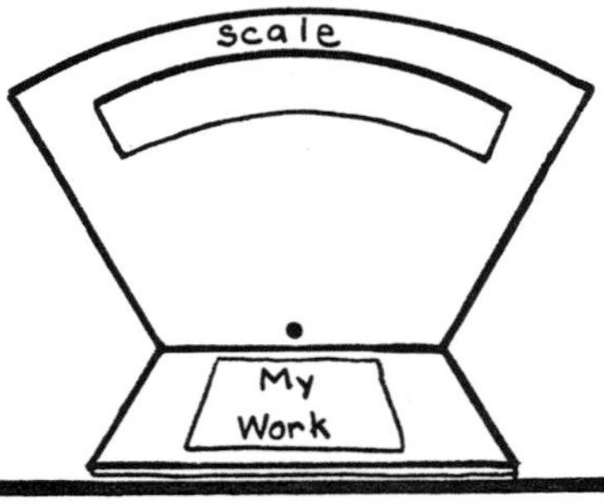

scale

My Work

name _____

date _____

I am learning about Nutrition.

Today I did the _____

_____ activity.

My work was:

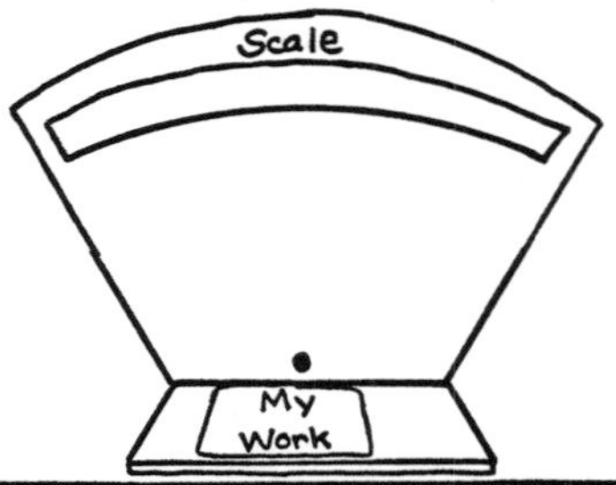

Scale

My Work

Nutrition Evaluation Page

name

Nutrition: Pizza Enrichment Page

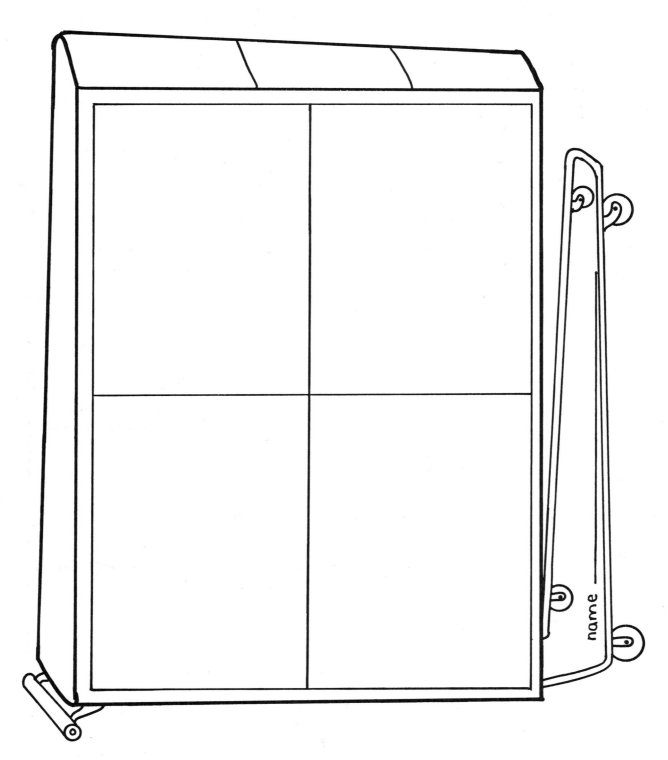

name

Nutrition: Shopping Enrichment Page

Words About:

name

Nutrition: Vocabulary Enrichment Page

Unit 3
BIRDS

ALL ABOUT BIRDS

Date _____

Dear Parent,

During the next two weeks our science unit will be about birds. Your child will learn a simple fact about birds at each activity area in addition to participating in the activity. He or she will copy it on a strip of paper, read it, and staple it onto a huge nest on our bulletin board.

Your child will make a bird feeder out of a clean, empty one-half gallon milk carton. The bird feeder will contain corn and sunflower seeds that your child will have carefully counted. Please help your child find a suitable place to hang his or her bird feeder.

At one of our activity areas the students will do feather experiments. Please send bird feathers which the students can share.

Your child will make a nesting bag as one of the activities. He or she will need a small mesh bag such as the kind used for onions, potatoes, or oranges with at least one-quarter inch holes.

As a group activity on _____ we will prepare food for the
                                                    date
birds. We will need pine cones for this project.

Please send bird feathers, cotton, scraps of material, a mesh bag, an empty one-half gallon milk carton, and pine cones as soon as possible for the bird activities.

Thank you for your continued support.

Sincerely,

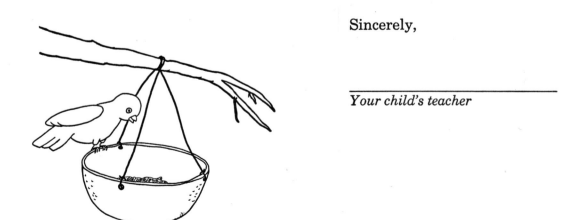

_____
Your child's teacher

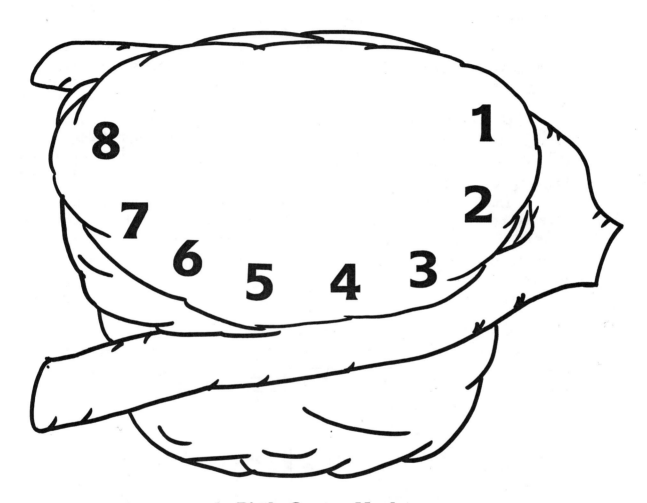

Birds Center Marker

BIRDS CENTER MARKER

A learning center marker is provided for students using the science unit activities at learning centers. (Refer to p. 246)

Distribute copies of the bird nest marker to the students. The student draws a bird in the nest. The students can cut out their markers and place them near the Bird Learning Centers.

TEACHER'S DIRECTIONS FOR THE OVERALL BIRDS ACTIVITIES

On the top of each file folder directions page is a fact about birds. Each bird activity relates to that fact. At each activity area is a container of 2-by-9-inch blank light brown construction paper strips (or recycled grocery bags cut into 2-by-9-inch strips). You may wish to color the facts brown at the top of each file folder directions page before you laminate them.

The first thing a student does upon arriving at the activity area is write the fact on a 2-by-9-inch paper, then proceed with the other file folder activities. The fact in the following illustration is "Birds have feathers."

When the student moves to the reading table, he or she takes the strip and finished activity work. The student reads his or her fact at the reading table to the other members of the reading group.

Sample facts appear on the bulletin board. Staple the student's fact strips daily to the giant nest on the bulletin board, as shown here

We are learning about birds.

1. Birds have feathers
2. Birds have many parts.
3. Birds lay eggs.
4. Birds eat often.
5. Some birds do not fly.
6. Birds are different sizes.
7. Birds have beaks.
8. Most birds build nests.

At the end of eight days of bird activities, the nest on the bulletin board is filled with strips and the students are filled with knowledge about birds.

BIRDS ACTIVITIES LIST

These activities emphasize eight facts about birds.

1. Birds Have Feathers Activity

Content areas: Science, handwriting

Skills: Experimenting, matching, observing, communicating, sorting, fine-motor coordination

Activities:

a. Sort the collection of feathers.
b. Look at the feathers with a microscope or magnifying glass, then label parts of the feather on the student activity page.
c. Do the feather waterproofing experiment.

2. Birds Have Many Parts Activity

Content areas: Science, handwriting, art, reading

Skills: Observing, creating, fine-motor coordination, using reference materials.

Activities:
a. Write the names of the bird parts on the overhead projector.
b. Draw a bird and label its parts.

3. Birds Lay Eggs Activity (Open-ended activity)

Content areas: Teacher's choice, handwriting

Skills: Fine-motor coordination, teacher's choice, using reference materials, matching

Activities:
a. Make an egg game.
b. Play the egg game with a friend.

4. Birds Eat Often Activity

Content areas: Science, math

Skills: Experimenting, counting, creating, fine-motor coordination

Activities:
a. Make a milk carton bird feeder.
b. Count 50 sunflower seeds into a bag.
c. Count 50 kernels of corn into a mortar and use a pestel to crack them. Put corn into a bag.

5. Some Birds Do Not Fly Activity

Content areas: Science, reading, art

Skills: Listening, creating, fine-motor coordination, using reference materials

Activities:
a. Listen to the cassette tape of the book.
b. Make a penguin out of construction paper.

6. Birds Are Different Sizes Activity

Content areas: Handwriting, art, reading

Skills: Creating, creative writing, using reference materials, communicating, observing, fine-motor coordination

Activities:

a. Write a story about a bird using references.

b. Paint a picture of the bird.

7. Birds Have Beaks Activity

Content areas: Science, art

Skills: Matching, sorting, fine-motor, classifying

Activities:

a. Sort and match the teacher-made bird cards.

b. Make a bird card game and an envelope.

8. Most Birds Build Nests Activity

Content areas: Science, reading, art, handwriting

Skills: Classifying, communicating, creating, fine-motor coordination, creative writing, using reference materials

Activities:

a. Make a book about nests.

b. Make a nesting bag.

TEACHER'S DIRECTIONS FOR THE BIRDS HAVE FEATHERS ACTIVITY

Content areas: Science, handwriting

Skills: Experimenting, matching, observing, communicating, sorting, fine-motor coordination

Materials needed:

    Copies of student activity page
    A collection of down and contour feathers
    Two containers for feathers
    Microscope or magnifying glass
    A container of water
    A container of salad oil
    Pencil
    One envelope per student

Materials preparation:

1. Establish background information about bird feathers including contour and down. Some good books are: Cole, Joanna, *A Bird's Body,* William Morrow and Co., New York, 1982; Freedman, Russell, *How Birds Fly,* Holiday House, New York, 1977; Garelick, May, *What Makes a Bird a Bird?,* Follett Publishing Co., New York, 1969. An excellent book about waterproofing feathers is Goldin, Augusta, *Ducks Don't Get Wet,* Thomas Y. Crowell Co., New York, 1965.

2. Make an example student activity page (refer to p. 109) with the webs, barb, shaft, and quill labelled for a student reference.

DIRECTIONS FOR FILE FOLDER ACTIVITIES

Activity 1

The student sorts the collection of feathers into two containers labelled "contour" and "down."

Activity 2

The student looks at the feathers with a microscope or magnifying glass. He or she draws the feather he or she saw in the lens on the student activity page. The student writes the parts of a feather referring to your example page.

Activity 3

The student does a feather experiment to show that the feathers of some birds, such as ducks, are waterproof:

1. The student sprinkles water on a feather.
2. He or she dips his or her fingers in the salad oil. Then the student pulls a feather through his or her fingers about three times until the feather is coated with oil.
3. The student sprinkles water on the oiled feather. He or she observes that the oiled feather stays dry because oil and water do not mix.
4. The student puts the waterproof feather into an envelope with his or her name on it.

Optional activity:

The student may want to sort the feather collection by matching sizes, color, and so on.

Birds have feathers

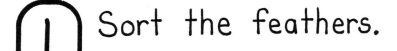

1 Sort the feathers.

feathers

 contour 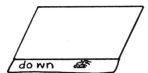 down

2 Look at the feather.
Do the ditto.

Feathers

shaft
barb
hook

name

3 Waterproof a feather.

oil

water

1. Sprinkle
   on water.

2. Rub on oil.

3. Sprinkle on
   water again.

File Folder Directions

Feathers

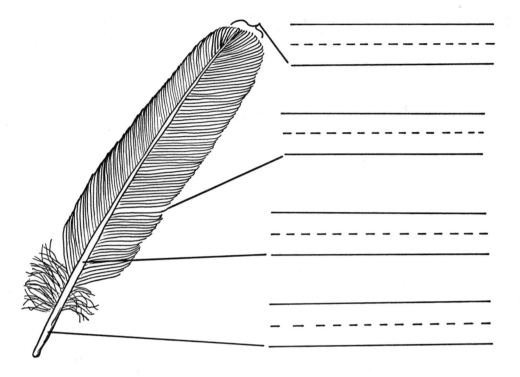

_____
- - - - - - - - - - -
_____

_____
- - - - - - - - - - -
_____

_____
- - - - - - - - - - -
_____

_____
- - - - - - - - - - -
_____

↙ Draw the feather
you magnified here.
Draw a line to
these parts:
shaft
barb
hook

name _____

Student Activity Page

TEACHER'S DIRECTIONS FOR THE BIRDS HAVE MANY PARTS ACTIVITY

Content areas: Science, handwriting, art, reading

Skills: Observing, creating, fine-motor coordination, using reference materials

Materials needed:

> Overhead projector and screen
> Marking pen for overhead transparency
> Teacher-made transparency of the teacher's direction page
> Bird books
> Paper
> Pencil
> Crayons

Materials preparation:

1. Make a transparency of the teacher's direction page to use on an overhead projector.
2. If an overhead projector is unavailable, make an enlarged drawing of the teacher's direction page on a chalkboard. The student writes the name of the bird parts using a copy of the teacher's direction page as a reference.

DIRECTIONS FOR FILE FOLDER ACTIVITIES

Activity 1

The student writes the names of the bird parts on the overhead projector transparency with a marking pen.

Activity 2

The student draws a bird with crayons on paper, using references. You may want to have the student draw the bird for your state. Then he or she labels the parts of the bird using the teacher's direction page as a reference.

Parts of a bird

_____

‑ ‑ ‑ ‑ ‑ ‑ ‑ ‑ ‑ ‑ ‑ ‑ ‑ ‑ ‑

_____

eye _____

‑ ‑ ‑ ‑ ‑ ‑ ‑ ‑ ‑

_____

crown _____

‑ ‑ ‑ ‑ ‑ ‑ ‑ ‑ ‑

_____

back _____

‑ ‑ ‑ ‑ ‑ ‑ ‑ ‑ ‑

_____

beak _____

‑ ‑ ‑ ‑ ‑ ‑ ‑ ‑ ‑

_____

wing _____

‑ ‑ ‑ ‑ ‑ ‑ ‑ ‑ ‑

_____

breast _____

‑ ‑ ‑ ‑ ‑ ‑ ‑ ‑ ‑

_____

claw _____

‑ ‑ ‑ ‑ ‑ ‑ ‑ ‑ ‑

_____

tail _____

‑ ‑ ‑ ‑ ‑ ‑ ‑ ‑ ‑

_____

leg _____

‑ ‑ ‑ ‑ ‑ ‑ ‑ ‑ ‑

_____

Student's name

_____

‑ ‑ ‑ ‑ ‑ ‑ ‑ ‑ ‑ ‑ ‑ ‑ ‑ ‑ ‑

_____

Teacher Direction Page

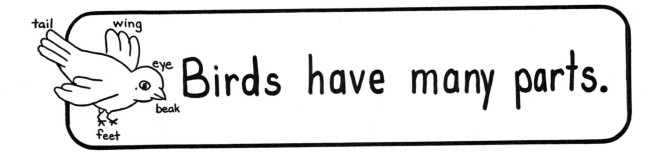

Birds have many parts.

① Write the parts of a bird.

② Draw a bird.
Label its parts.

File Folder Directions

TEACHER'S DIRECTIONS FOR BIRDS LAY EGGS ACTIVITY

Content areas: Teacher's choice (refer to page **x**), handwriting

Skills: Fine-motor coordination, teacher's choice, using reference materials, matching

Materials needed:

Teacher-made egg game
Copies of two student activity pages (ditto on heavy paper)
Pencil
Scissors
One brass fastener one-half-inch long per student

Materials preparation:

1. Establish background that birds lay eggs. Some good books are Cole, Joanna, *A Chick Hatches,* William Morrow and Co., New York, 1976; Isenbart, Hans-Heinrich, *A Duckling is Born,* G. P. Putnam's Sons, New York, 1981; Selsam, Millicent, *Egg to Chick,* Harper and Row, New York, 1970.
2. Make an egg game as pictured on the file folder directions page. Determine a skill you wish to reinforce or review such as math problems and answers. After you have assembled and connected the Egg and Egg Wheel student activity pages write one math problem in the cut-out opening at the left edge of the egg. Continue to write a different math problem in the cut-out opening as you carefully rotate the egg wheel. (Match the dashed lines of the egg wheel with the cut-out opening). You may want to write the answer to one problem under the answer flap on the egg for an example.

DIRECTIONS FOR FILE FOLDER ACTIVITIES

Activity 1

The student makes his or her own egg game referring to your sample.

Activity 2

The student plays the egg game with a friend.

Birds lay eggs.

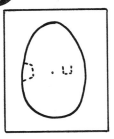**1** Make the egg game.

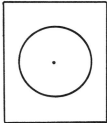 

2 Play the game with a friend.

File Folder Directions

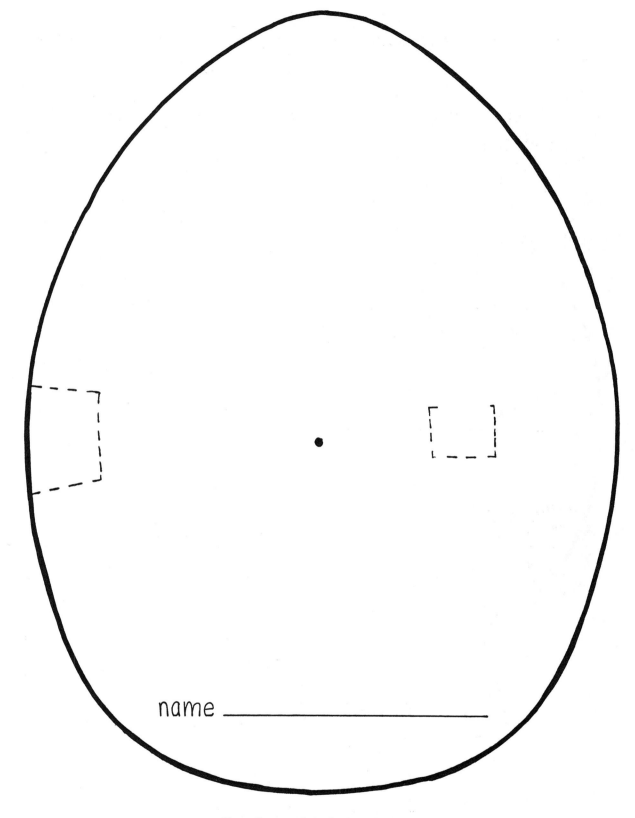

name _____

Student Activity Page

Egg Wheel

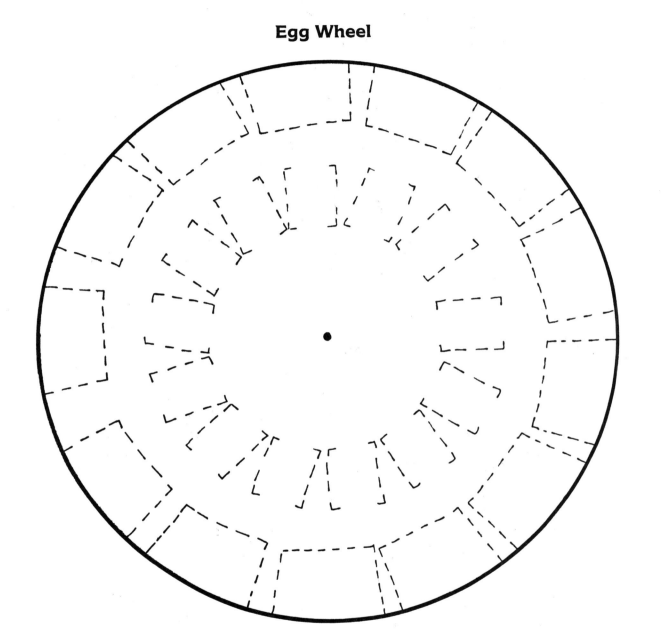

Student Activity Page

TEACHER'S DIRECTIONS FOR THE BIRDS EAT OFTEN ACTIVITY

Content areas: Science, math

Skills: Experimenting, counting, creating, fine-motor coordination

Materials needed:

> Teacher-made milk-carton bird feeder
> Teacher-made posterboard pattern
> One-half gallon milk carton per student
> One pipe cleaner per student
> Two small plastic bags and ties per student
> 50 sunflower seeds per student
> 50 kernels of corn per student
> Crayons
> Scissors
> Two containers for seeds
> Mortar and pestel (or stone and sturdy wooden bowl)

Materials preparation:

> Make a pattern and a milk-carton bird feeder as pictured in the file folder directions.

DIRECTIONS FOR FILE FOLDER ACTIVITIES

Activity 1

The student lays the pattern on the milk carton about one inch from the bottom. He or she traces around the pattern on the milk carton with a crayon. The student cuts out the flap and pokes holes in the top of the carton with scissors, then pushes the pipe cleaner through the hole and ties it.

Activity 2

The student carefully counts 50 sunflower seeds into a small bag and ties it. The student counts 50 kernels of corn into a mortar and uses a pestel to crack them. He or she puts the corn into a small plastic bag and ties it. (Encourage students to hang their bird feeders at home and maintain the feeders.)

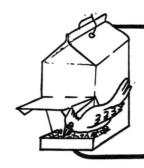

Birds eat often.

1 Make a bird feeder.

pipe cleaner

pattern

2 Count 50 sunflower seeds.

tie

Count 50 kernels of corn.
Crack the corn.

tie

File Folder Directions

TEACHER'S DIRECTIONS FOR THE SOME BIRDS DO NOT FLY ACTIVITY

Content areas: Science, reading, art

Skills: Listening, creating, fine-motor coordination, using reference materials

Materials needed:

> One sheet of 9-by-12-inch black construction paper per student
> One sheet of 5½-by-6-inch white construction paper per student
> One sheet of 3-by-3-inch yellow construction paper per student
> One sheet of 3-by-6-inch white construction paper per student
> One sheet of 3-by-3-inch orange construction paper per student
> Pencil
> Scissors
> Paste
> Tape recorder
> Cassette tape
> A book about penguins such as Bonners, Susan, *A Penguin Year,* Delacorte Press, New York, 1981; Freeman, Don, *Penguins of All People,* The Viking Press, New York, 1971; Hutchins, Ross E., *Adelbert the Penguin,* Rand McNally and Co., New York, 1969; Serventy, Vincent, *Animals in the Wild-Penguin,* Scholastic, Inc., New York, 1983.

Materials preparation:

1. Tape record the book you have chosen for this activity.
2. Make an example penguin as pictured on the file folder directions.
3. Establish background about penguins. Some good books are *Mizumura, Kazue, The Emperor Penguins,* Thomas Y. Crowell Co., New York, 1969; Stonehouse, Bernard, *Penguins,* McGraw-Hill Book Co., New York, 1979; Tenaza, Richard, *Penguins,* Franklin Watts, New York, 1980.
4. Discuss with the students: Why do you think penguins cannot fly? How do they get around? Where do they live? What other birds cannot fly?

DIRECTIONS FOR FILE FOLDER ACTIVITIES

Activity 1

The student listens to the cassette tape of the book.

Activity 2

The student uses construction paper, pencil, scissors, and paste to make a penguin referring to your example.

Optional activity

The students may want to put their penguins on a bulletin board to form a rookery.

Some birds do not fly.

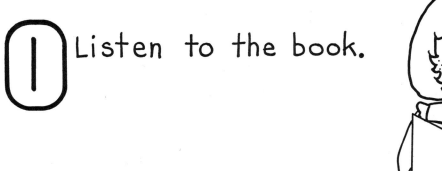

1 | Listen to the book.

2 | Make a penguin.

black

white

yellow
beak

orange
2 feet

wing | wing

body

eyes

belly

Paste

fold

File Folder Directions

TEACHER'S DIRECTIONS FOR THE BIRDS ARE DIFFERENT SIZES ACTIVITY

Content areas: Handwriting, art, reading

Skills: Creating, creative writing, using reference materials, communicating, observing, fine-motor coordination

Materials needed:

> Paint
> Paintbrushes
> Easel
> Paper
> Pencil
> References: pictionary, dictionary, bird books

Materials preparation:

> Display several bird books. In addition, you may want to use audiovisual aids to establish background information about different sizes of birds such as ostriches, herons, flamingos, hummingbirds, and wrens.

DIRECTIONS FOR FILE FOLDER ACTIVITIES

Activity 1

> The student writes a story about a bird using references. (Encourage them to write about size, color, habitat, food, and so on.)

Activity 2

The student paints a picture of the bird.

Birds are different sizes.

1 Write a bird story.

2 Paint the bird.

File Folder Directions

TEACHER'S DIRECTIONS FOR THE BIRDS HAVE BEAKS ACTIVITY

Content areas: Science, art

Skills: Matching, sorting, fine-motor coordination, classifying

Materials needed:

> Copies of the student activity page
> Crayons
> Pencil
> Scissors
> Paste
> One sheet of 12-by-18-inch paper per student
> Teacher-made bird cards

Materials preparation:

Use 3-by-5-inch index cards to make a set of bird cards as pictured on the file folder directions.

1. You will need four beak picture cards, four word category cards (seed eater, meat eater, fruit eater, insect eater), and two bird pictures for each of these categories: seed eaters—bluejay, cardinal, sparrow, chickadee; meat eaters—owl, hawk, eagle, falcon; fruit eaters—catbird, starling, mockingbird, thrasher; insect eaters—bluebird, meadowlark, robin, woodpecker.
2. You may want to color code the back of the cards for each category such as a red dot for the seed eater cards, and so on.
3. Laminate the cards and provide a container for them.
4. Prepare an area for this activity such as a bulletin board (tack the beak and category cards on it) or a magnetic chalkboard (glue a magnet to the back of each card, so the card can stick to the chalkboard).

DIRECTIONS FOR FILE FOLDER ACTIVITIES

Activity 1

The student sorts and matches the teacher-made bird cards into the appropriate categories.

Activity 2

1. The student makes a bird card game as pictured on the file folder directions:

    a. The student folds the paper into an eight-box format.

    b. He or she writes the names of the four categories on the paper.

    c. The student chooses a bird from each category to draw opposite the name of the category.

    d. He or she cuts each category section differently making the game self-checking.

2. The student colors, cuts, folds, and pastes the sides of the Bird Beaks student activity page to form an envelope. The student writes his or her name on it.

3. The student can play the game alone or with a friend.

4. Optional: the older student may want to make an additional set of cards featuring four more birds.

Birds have beaks.

Match the birds and the beaks.

1

seed eater	meat eater	fruit eater	insect eater

2 Make a game and envelope.

seed eater	
meat eater	
fruit eater	
insect eater	

Bird Beaks

seed eater | meat eater | fruit eater | insect eater

Paste

File Folder Directions

Bird Beaks

seed eater   meat eater   fruit eater   insect eater

fold

name

Student Activity Page

TEACHER'S DIRECTIONS FOR THE MOST BIRDS BUILD NESTS ACTIVITY

Content areas: Science, reading, art, handwriting

Skills: Classifying, communicating, creating, fine-motor coordination, creative writing, using reference materials

Materials needed:

Paper (wallpaper, notebook, handwriting, construction)

Pencil

Crayons

Stapler and staples

Scissors

One pipe cleaner per student

One small mesh bag (the kind used for packaging onions, potatoes, or oranges with at least ¼-inch holes) per student

A collection of string, yarn, cotton batting, fabric scraps, ribbon, and leaves in a container

Teacher-made book

Materials preparation:

You may want to use the following books to establish background information about bird nests: Gans, Roma, *It's Nesting Time,* Thomas Y. Crowell Co., New York, 1964; Shackelford, Nina and Burks, Gordon E., *Bird Nests,* Golden Press, Inc., New York, 1962.

Make an example book for the students to copy, emphasizing nesting locations and patterning. Some ideas are:

1. "A hole is the best nest for a _____," (on the front side of the paper) "But not for a _____." (on the back side of the paper).
2. "A tree is the best nest for a _____," (on the front side of the paper) "But not for a _____." (on the back side of the paper).
3. "The ground is the best nest for a _____," (on the front side of the paper) "But not for a _____." (on the back side of the paper).

In preparing the books, you need to determine:

1. The number of pages in the book (older students can do several).
2. The type of paper you will use for the cover and content pages.
3. How to assemble the books, using your book as reference:
   a. Older students may put together the cover and content pages, staple the book together, write the book, and illustrate it.
   b. You may prefer to staple a book together yourself for younger students, then they can write the book and illustrate it.

Prepare a collection of nesting materials such as string, yarn, cotton batting, fabric scraps, ribbon, and leaves in a container. You may want to make a nesting bag. Fill a small mesh bag about three-quarters-full of small pieces of nesting materials. Weave and tie the bag shut with a pipe cleaner. The students can hang their bags to trees in the Spring.

DIRECTIONS FOR FILE FOLDER ACTIVITIES

Activity 1

The student assembles his or her book according to the book directions. Then he or she writes and illustrates the pages.

Activity 2

The student makes a nesting bag referring to your example.

Follow-up activity

Encourage the students to hang their bags in trees near their homes. The students should look around their home area to see if they can spot any of their materials in a nest.

Most birds build nests.

1 Make a book about nests.

2 Make a nesting bag.

nesting materials

File Folder Directions

Birds
Enrichment Activities

TEACHER'S SUGGESTIONS FOR BIRDS ENRICHMENT ACTIVITIES

1. Birds Group Activity (refer to pp. 133–38)

Bird Treats

2. Birds Home Study (refer to p. 139)

Ditto the page on colored paper. Encourage students to watch birds and keep a record of them. You may want to establish background for this activity by having the students watch and identify birds at your school location. Use a field guide to identify birds in your area such as the books referred to on the Bird Home Study page. You may want to obtain a checklist of birds for your area from the National Audubon Society, 950 Third Avenue, New York, N.Y., 10022. Another excellent source is: Kress, Stephen W., *The Audubon Society Handbook for Birders*, Charles Scribner's Sons, New York, 1981. You may want to compile a class list of the birds identified when the data is returned.

3. Birds Award (refer to p. 141)

Ditto the page on colored paper. Give each child who returns the Home Study Bird Watcher List a Home Study Award. The Birds Award may be used for the recognition of good work and so on.

4. Birds Evaluation (refer to p. 142)

The evaluations may be stapled to the students bird related work. The grade may be based on a joint teacher-student decision. The student traces the dashed line with a crayon to indicate the appropriate length of his or her performance level. (The lowest level is closest to the small bird.)

5. Food for the Birds (refer to p. 143)

This page may be used following the Bird Treats activity. The student may write about each of the four kinds of foods he or she prepared. The student may want to list the ingredients for each of the four foods prepared. He or she may want to draw pictures of the four foods prepared.

6. Birds Bingo (refer to p. 144)

The student copies the names of 16 birds in random order from the chalk-board onto his or her Bingo card. After all of the students have made Bingo cards, play Bingo. You or a designated student calls the bird names and the students cover the words called with paper markers. The winner needs to cover four words in a row or four corners. The winner may be the next caller for the game.

7. Birds Stamp (refer to p. 145)

The student designs a bird stamp on this page. You may wish to display bird pictures, books, and so on for references.

8. Birds Webbed Feet (refer to p. 146)

This page may be used for creative writing, "If I had webbed feet . . . "

GROUP ACTIVITIES

As a culminating activity to the Birds science unit, schedule a Bird Treats project. Each student will make four kinds of simple bird feeders containing bird treats.

Prior to the Bird Treat project, send a letter to parents requesting help and ingredients. You may use the letter provided earlier in this unit.

The parents who will help with the project can bring in utensils such as table knives, sharp knives, spoons for stirring, thread, embroidery or darning needles, and whatever else your class needs for the project.

On the day that you make Bird Treats, help the parents set up four different areas in your room with the necessary ingredients for the recipes (ingredients to follow). One or two parents should be sufficient to help per group. They will need to give close supervision to the students that are carefully using darning needles.

When you are ready to begin the Bird Treats activity, let the parents pop enough popcorn for the students to eat and to string. They will also need to cut oranges into halves. During the same period of time, the students may design place mats on 12-by-18-inch paper. They can also decorate a large paper bag with their name and bird pictures on it. (The bag will be used to carry the four different Bird Treats.)

Next, let each student eat the popcorn and one-half of an orange on his or her place mat. (You may also want to serve a beverage.) The student will need to save the orange shell for a bird feeder.

After the students finish eating and cleaning up, divide them into four small groups. The students will rotate to the four different areas to make the bird treats and put them into their bags. You may want to make and display recipe charts at each of the four areas.

The following recipes are suggested for the Bird Treats activity. You may want to try other recipes. Some good references are: Cosgrove, Irene E. and Ed, *My Recipes Are For The Birds,* Doubleday and Co., Inc., Garden City, N.Y., 1975; Crook, Beverly Courtney, *Invite a Bird to Dinner,* Lothrop, Lee and Shepherd Co., New York, 1978.

Please note that the students will be making the Bird Treats recipes under adult supervision (approximately one adult per six students).

"Popcorn String-A-Lings"

Each student will need:

> 1 large embroidery or darning needle
>
> 1 piece of 24-inch heavy thread
>
> 1 cup of popped popcorn (approximately)
>
> 1/4 cup of raisins (approximately)
>
> 1/4 cup of cranberries (approximately)

Step 1:
> Thread a needle with heavy thread and tie a knot at the end of it.

Step 2:
> Use the needle to thread the popcorn, cranberries, and raisins onto the heavy thread. (You may want to encourage the students to count the popcorn, cranberries, and raisins, then thread them in a pattern.)

"Pine Cone Whirligigs"

Each student will need:

> 2 pine cones (medium size)
>
> 1 piece of 24-inch string
>
> 1 table knife
>
> 2 tablespoons creamy peanut butter
>
> 1 1/2 tablespoons cornmeal
>
> 1 tablespoon
>
> 1 small bowl such as a margarine tub
>
> 1 plastic bag (1 gallon size)

Step 1:

> Tie one pine cone near the middle (12″) and one pine cone at the end of the string.

Step 2:

> Blend the cornmeal and the peanut butter in a bowl with a tablespoon.

Step 3:

> Spread the peanut butter mixture with a table knife onto the pine cones filling the crevices.

Step 4:

> Put the string of pine cones into a small plastic bag.

"Peanut Swingers"

Each student will need:

> 1 large embroidery or darning needle
> 1 piece of 24-inch heavy thread
> 10 unshelled peanuts

Step 1:

> Thread a needle with a heavy thread and tie a knot at the end of it.

Step 2:

> Thread 10 unshelled peanuts one at a time on the heavy thread.

"Orange Hideaways"

Each student will need:

> ½ of an orange shell
> 1 large embroidery or darning needle
> Three 12-inch pipe cleaners
> 20 raisins (approximately)
> 4 tablespoons creamy peanut butter
> 3½ tablespoons cornmeal
> ¼ cup wild bird seed
> 1 small bowl such as a margarine tub
> 1 tablespoon
> 1 plastic bag (one gallon size)
> Ruler
> Scissors

Step 1:

> Use the needle to poke three holes in the orange shell as pictured on the opening page for this unit.

Step 2:

Put the pipe cleaners through the holes and twist them above the edge of the orange shell. Twist the opposite ends of the three pipe cleaners together to form a hanger.

Step 3:

Blend the cornmeal and peanut butter in a bowl with a tablespoon, then add the wildbird seed and raisins.

Step 4:

Fill the orange shell with the mixture.

Step 5:

Put the orange shell feeder into a small plastic bag.

Follow-up Activities:

1. Encourage the students to have someone in their family help them hang up the feeders in an appropriate area. The students may refill the orange shell and the pine cones when they become empty. The students should also set out a container of water for the birds.

2. The "Food for Birds" enrichment page may be used to list the recipes.

IT'S FOR THE BIRDS!

Date _____

Dear Parent,

We will culminate our Birds science unit on _____ at

_____ with a Bird Treats group activity.

day

time

Your child will make four different kinds of bird feeders. Please help your child find a good location to hang his or her feeders. Also set out a container of water for the birds.

On the following page is a list of the items we will need for the bird treats. Please decide which items you would be willing to contribute and return the list to me by _____. I will notify you which of the items you should

day

send to school.

We will be popping popcorn. If you are willing to share a popcorn popper with us, please indicate that on the list.

We will need several parents to help make the bird treats. If you would like to help, please check that on the list.

Thank you for your continued support.

Sincerely,

_____

Your child's teacher

(Your child's name)_____

      I would be willing to send in any of the following items I have checked for the Bird Treats activity:

_____ 1 lb. unpopped popcorn

_____ 1 small jar of creamy peanut butter

_____ 1 lb. cornmeal

_____ 1 lb. cranberries

_____ 1 lb. raisins

_____ 1 lb. unshelled peanuts

_____ 6 oranges

_____ 1 lb. wild bird seed

_____ 12 clean, empty margarine tubs

_____ 10 large grocery bags

_____ 50 plastic food storage bags (1 gallon size)

_____ 50 pine cones (medium size)

_____ I can send any *one* of the above ingredients.

_____ I can bring in my popcorn popper and cooking oil on _____
                                                     day

_____ I will come to school by _____on _____to help a small group
                                     time   *day*

of children make bird treats.

Signed: _____   Phone: _____

Please return this note by _____
                                     day

I will contact you for definite arrangements.

Bird Home Study
Enrichment Activity Page
Return by _____

Home Study

Date _____

Dear Parent,

　　We will begin a science unit about birds this week.

　　Please encourage your child to look for birds in your area and keep a record of them from _____ to _____ on the attached
　　　　　　　　　　　　　　　　date　　　　　　　　　*date*

Bird Watcher List. Return the list to school on _____.

　　It will be helpful to use a field guide to birds for your area, such as Peterson, Roger Tory, *A Field Guide to the Birds,* Houghton Mifflin, Boston, 1980 (all birds east of the Rocky Mountains) or Peterson, Roger Tory, *A Field Guide to Western Birds,* Houghton Mifflin, Boston, 1961 (all birds west of the Rocky Mountains). You may find these books at a library or bookstore.

　　Thank you for your help with this project.

Sincerely,

_____
Your child's teacher

I am a bird watcher.
I saw ___ different birds.

_____
(ornithologist's name)

_____'s Bird Watcher List
child's name

Return by _____
date

Bird's Name	Place	Date	Comments

I am a bird watcher.
I saw ___ different birds.

_____
(ornithologist's name)

Home Study Award

Who?
You are becoming
wise about birds.

_____
name

Birds Award

name _____
date _____

I am learning about birds.

My work was _____.

How high did you fly today?

name _____
date _____

8 1
7 2
6 5 4 3

I am learning about birds.
Today I learned that: _____
_____

How high did you fly today?

Birds Evaluation Page

Food for the Birds

1

2

3

4

name _____

Birds Enrichment Page

This bird stamp designed by:

_____

Birds: Stamp Enrichment Page

If I had
webbed feet...

Birds: Webbed Feet Enrichment Page

Unit 4
TREES

TERRIFIC TREES

Date _____

Dear Parent,

Trees will be the theme of our science unit activities beginning next week. We will study different kinds of trees, parts of trees, tree products, tree growth, and so on.

Encourage your child to collect leaves and press them in a magazine or catalog and bring them to school. Your child will use the leaves to create leaf rubbing "creatures."

As one of the art activities your child will create a tree house. Please help all of our tree house "builders" by sending unwanted items (small boxes, cardboard tubes, cardboard strips, popsicle sticks, straws, and tongue depressors) for this activity.

Anticipate receiving a large tree poster. Please find a place to display it because your child will have worked hard labeling the parts of the tree. You may want to extend this activity by showing your child different evergreen and deciduous trees in your area. He or she may identify the parts of the trees.

If you have cross-cut sections of a tree that our class may borrow for this unit, please contact me this week.

Our group activity will be a "Save a Tree" day on _____.
date

We will emphasize re-cycling: You can help at home by encouraging your family to recycle items.

Thank you for your continued support.

Sincerely,

_____
Your child's teacher

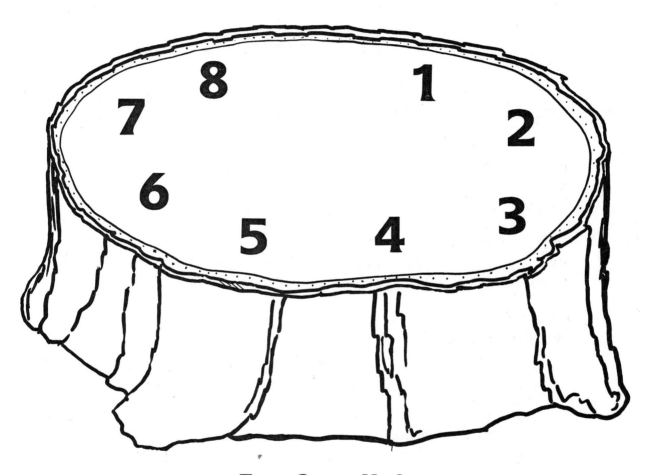

Trees Center Marker

TREES CENTER MARKER

A learning center marker is provided for students using the science unit activities at learning centers. (refer to p. 246)

Distribute copies of the preceding tree stump marker to the students. The students can cut out their markers and place them near the Trees Learning Centers.

TREES ACTIVITIES LIST

These activities relate to various aspects of trees, including, kinds of trees, parts of trees, stages of tree growth, products, and fruits.

1. **Parts of Trees Activity** (a bulletin board is used with this activity)

   Content areas: Science, art

   Skills: Classifying, matching, creating, fine-motor coordination, using reference materials

   Activities:

   a. Match the cards to the tree parts on the bulletin board.

   b. Make a tree poster.

2. **Nuts Activity** (Open-ended activity)

   Content areas: Science, teacher's choice, handwriting

   Skills: Sorting, matching, fine-motor coordination, teacher's choice

   Activities:

   a. Sort the nuts.

   b. Match the acorns and caps.

3. **Tree Products Activity**

   Content areas: Science, reading

   Skills: Sorting, classifying, using reference materials, communicating, fine-motor coordination

   Activities:

   a. Find eight tree products in the assortment of objects.

   b. Write the products and illustrate them.

4. **Tree House Activity**

   Content areas: Handwriting, art

Skills: Creating, creative writing, communicating, fine-motor coordination

Activities:

a. Make a tree house out of junk materials.
b. Write about your tree house.

5. Colorful Tree Tour Activity

Content areas: Science, reading

Skills: Classifying, communicating, creating, using reference materials, fine-motor coordination

6. Apples Activity

Content areas: Reading, art, science

Skills: Listening, creating, experimenting

Activities:

a. Listen to the story about apples.
b. Paint an apple tree.

7. Tree Growth Activity

Content areas: Science, reading, math

Skills: Predicting, communicating, sorting, measuring, observing, classifying, creating, fine-motor coordination, sequencing

Activities:

a. Sort and sequence the examples of growth stages.
b. Draw and compare a growing tree and yourself on the student activity page.

8. Leaf Creatures Activity

Content areas: Science, art

Skills: Experimenting, creating, communicating, observing, fine-motor coordination, creative writing

Activities:

a. Make leaf rubbings.
b. Change the rubbings into creatures.

TEACHER'S DIRECTIONS FOR THE PARTS OF TREES ACTIVITY

Content areas: Science, art

Skills: Classifying, matching, creating, fine-motor coordination, using reference materials

Materials needed:

> Bulletin board
> Pencil
> One piece of 12-by-18-inch heavy paper per student
> Crayons
> Thumbtacks and container
> Teacher-made parts of trees cards
> Teacher-made tree reference charts

Materials preparation:

1. Establish background information about two classifications of trees, evergreens and deciduous. Some good books are: Brandt, Keith, *Discovering Trees,* Troll Associates, Mahwah, N.J., 1982; Dowden, Anne Ophelia, *The Blossom on the Bough: A Book of Trees,* Thomas Y. Crowell Co., New York, 1975; Kirkpatrick, Rena K., *Look at Trees,* Macdonald-Raintree Inc., Milwaukee, 1978.

2. Prepare a bulletin board as pictured in the file folder directions. Put yellow stickers or circles of construction paper (approximately one-half inch diameter) on appropriate parts of the evergreen tree. Use red stickers or circles of construction paper to indicate tree part locations on the deciduous tree.

3. Make parts-of-a-tree cards. Use a black water-base marking pen and 3-by-5-inch index cards to make the following set of parts-of-an-evergreen cards: leaf, branch, seed, trunk, roots, and bark. Color code the back of the cards with a yellow dot to correspond with the circles on the evergreen on the bulletin board. Make a duplicate set of cards for the deciduous tree. Color code the back of these cards with a red dot to correspond with the red circles on the deciduous tree. Laminate the cards and an envelope for them.

4. Make an evergreen chart and a deciduous chart with the parts of the tree listed on them. You may want to include pictures of the parts for the younger student.

DIRECTIONS FOR FILE FOLDER ACTIVITIES

Activity 1

The student tacks the parts-of-the-tree cards to the corresponding location on each of the trees on the bulletin board.

Activity 2

The student makes a tree poster:

1. He or she folds a large piece of paper in half.
2. The student uses crayons to draw the roots below the fold of the paper.
3. He or she draws the other parts of the tree above the fold of the paper.
4. The student labels the parts of the tree referring to your tree charts.
5. Optional: The older student may make an evergreen tree on the front side of the poster and a deciduous tree on the opposite side of it.

Parts of Trees

1 Match the cards to the tree parts.

Parts of Trees

evergreen   deciduous

cards

2 Make a tree poster. Label the parts.

Crayons

trunk

roots

File Folder Directions

TEACHER'S DIRECTIONS FOR THE NUTS ACTIVITY

Content areas: Science, teacher's choice (refer to page **x**), handwriting

Skills: Sorting, matching, fine-motor coordination, teacher's choice

Materials needed:

> Copies of the student activity page
> Pencil
> Crayons
> Scissors
> Paste
> A collection of nuts
> Containers for the nuts
> A pair of tongs

Materials preparation:

1. Establish background information about acorns, and other kinds of nuts. Some books are: Glease, Hannah, *The Magic Tree And The Missing Acorn,* Ray Rourke Publishing Co., Inc., Windermere, Florida, 1981; Hutchins, Ross E., *Lives Of An Oak Tree,* Rand McNally, and Co., New York, 1962; Russell, Solveig, *About Nuts,* Melmont Publishers, Inc., Chicago, 1963.

2. Provide a collection of nuts such as acorns, walnuts, pecans, and hickory in a container. Determine the number of varieties and nuts to sort. Provide a labeled container for each variety.

3. Determine a skill you wish to reinforce or review. Some ideas are math problems, contractions, compound words, and so on. Make a reference chart for the students by writing the words or problems on the acorns on a copy of the student activity page. (The student will write the answer on an acorn cap that he or she will cut out and paste on the corresponding acorn.)

DIRECTIONS FOR FILE FOLDER ACTIVITIES

Activity 1

The student sorts the collection of nuts by using tongs, picking them up one at a time, and placing them into appropriate containers.

Activity 2

The student copies the reference chart on the student activity page and completes the work. He or she cuts out and pastes the cap to the corresponding acorn.

Nuts

1 Sort the nuts.

2 Match the acorns and caps.

File Folder Directions

Acorns and Caps

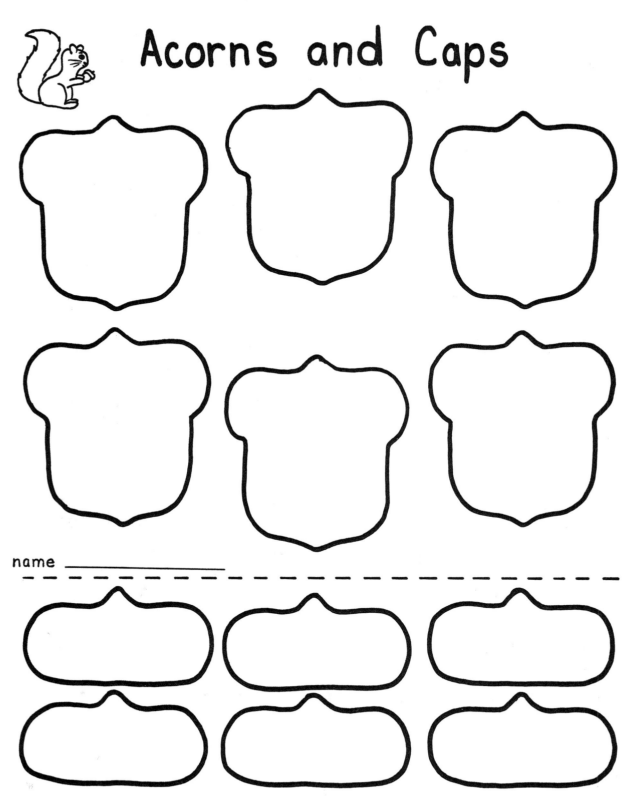

name _____

© 1988 by The Center for Applied Research in Education

Student Activity Page

TEACHER'S DIRECTIONS FOR THE TREE PRODUCTS ACTIVITY

Content areas: Science, reading

Skills: Sorting, classifying, using reference materials, communicating, fine-motor coordination

Materials needed:

>Paper
>Pencil
>Crayons
>References: dictionary, pictionary
>An assortment of several objects including at least eight items from tree products such as shoe polish, pencil, paper, maple syrup, book, magazine, newspaper, wooden doll furniture, wooden ruler, paint, wooden clothespin, and so on. Other assorted objects may include sponge, chalk, paper clip, pan, and so on.

Materials preparation:

1. Use books, audiovisual aids, and so on to establish background information about tree products.
2. Label the assortment of objects for the younger students.

DIRECTIONS FOR FILE FOLDER ACTIVITIES

Activity 1

The student sorts the array of objects to find eight tree products.

Activity 2

The student writes the names of the eight tree products on an eight-box format paper as pictured on the file folder directions page. Younger students may copy your labels, while older students should use references to write the names. He or she illustrates the tree products.

Optional activity

Older students may use references to find eight additional tree products to record and illustrate on the back of the paper.

Tree Products

1 Find 8 tree products.

Find 8
tree products.

2 Write the products.
Draw the pictures.

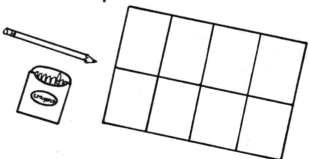

File Folder Directions

TEACHER'S DIRECTIONS FOR THE TREE HOUSE ACTIVITY

Content areas: Handwriting, art

Skills: Creating, creative writing, communicating, fine-motor coordination

Materials needed:

> Copies of the student activity page
> Pencil
> Crayons
> Scissors
> Glue
> Masking tape
> A collection of junk materials such as boxes of various sizes, cardboard tubes, tongue depressors, popsicle sticks, straws, cardboard strips, assorted colors, and sizes of construction paper.

Materials preparation:

> Discuss tree houses (construction, safety, uses, and so on) with the students.

DIRECTIONS FOR FILE FOLDER ACTIVITIES

Activity 1

The student uses junk materials to create a tree house.

Activity 2

The student writes a creative story on the student activity page about a tree house, such as "If I lived in a tree house. . . . " He or she illustrates the story.

Tree House

1 Make a tree house.

tree house materials

glue

2 Write about your house.

File Folder Directions

Student Activity Page

TEACHER'S DIRECTIONS FOR THE COLORFUL TREE TOUR ACTIVITY

Content areas: Science, reading

Skills: Classifying, communicating, creating, fine-motor coordination, using reference materials.

Materials needed:

> Copies of the student activity (ditto on heavy paper)
> One 9-by-4-inch envelope per student
> Crayons
> Scissors
> Pencil
> Teacher-made Colorful Tree Tour game

Materials preparation:

1. Select three deciduous trees common to your area for this activity. Establish background information about the seasonal changes of deciduous trees. Some good books are: Brandt, Keith, *Discovering Trees,* Troll Associates, Mahwah, New Jersey, 1982; Caufield, Peggy, *Leaves,* Coward, McCann and Geoghegan, Inc., New York, 1962; May, Julian, *Forests That Change Color,* Creative Educational Society, Inc., Mankato, Minnesota, 1972; Thomson, Ruth, *Usborne First Nature Trees,* EDC Publishing, Tulsa, Oklahoma. It will be helpful to use a field identification guide to prepare cards for the game. One guide that you may wish to use is: Brockman, C. Frank, *Trees of North America,* Western Publishing Co., Inc., Racine, Wis., 1968.

2. Prepare a Colorful Tree Tour game: (The game may be played in a variety of ways according to the ability level of your students.) Use a copy of the student activity page to make a gameboard:

   a. Write the names of the three trees that you have selected in random order on the "road" spaces. (You may want to write the names of the three trees on the student activity page prior to dittoing it for the younger student.)

   b. Color the "road" spaces yellow for one tree name, orange for another tree name, and red for the last tree name.

   c. Prepare tree facts on 3-by-5-inch index cards for the game. Use simple Rebus-style sentences for the younger student such as:

"I have _____." (Draw an acorn in the blank.) "My _____ has three points." (Draw a maple leaf in the blank.) "_____ like to eat my _____." (Draw squirrels and acorns in the blanks.)

Older student ideas are: "My seeds float through the air." "Syrup is made from my sap." "Squirrels like to bury my fruits." "I grow 80 to 100 feet tall." Write the answer at the bottom of the card. (You may wish to color code the cards for the younger student by putting a yellow dot for one tree name, orange for another, and red for the last tree name corresponding to the gameboard.)

d. Make a dittoed copy of the tree fact cards for each student. He or she may cut them apart to use as cards for his or her game. He or she may keep them in an envelope.

e. Laminate the gameboard and the cards.

f. Provide a container for the cards and two checkers or buttons for the game.

g. Game directions: The student plays the game with a friend. Each player puts his or her checker on "Start Here" on the gameboard. The players take turns drawing tree fact cards from the container. Player 1 draws a tree fact card from the container and reads it to Player 2. Player 2 guesses the name of the tree. Player 1 verifies the answer by reading the tree name or matching the color code at the bottom of the tree fact card. Player 2 advances to the nearest corresponding space on the gameboard if his or her answer is correct. The first player to reach "Finish Here" on the gameboard is the winner.

h. *Optional:* If you are teaching very young students you may wish to make the gameboard with three different colored "road" spaces. Make corresponding colored leaf-shaped cards of three different trees. Do not write any words on them. Play the game in the same manner as previously described. The students will learn to identify three trees by their leaf shapes. You may wish to make a reference chart with the three leaves labeled on it.

DIRECTIONS FOR FILE FOLDER ACTIVITIES

Activity 1

The student uses the student activity page to make a Colorful Tree Tour gameboard referring to your sample gameboard. He or she makes tree fact cards as per your directions.

Activity 2

The student plays the Colorful Tree Tour game with a friend.

Colorful Tree Tour

1 Make the tree game.

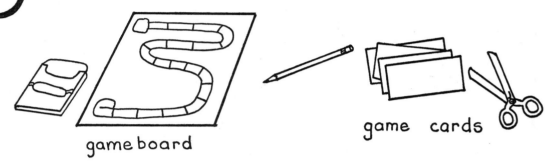

game board   game cards

2 Play the game with a friend.

File Folder Directions

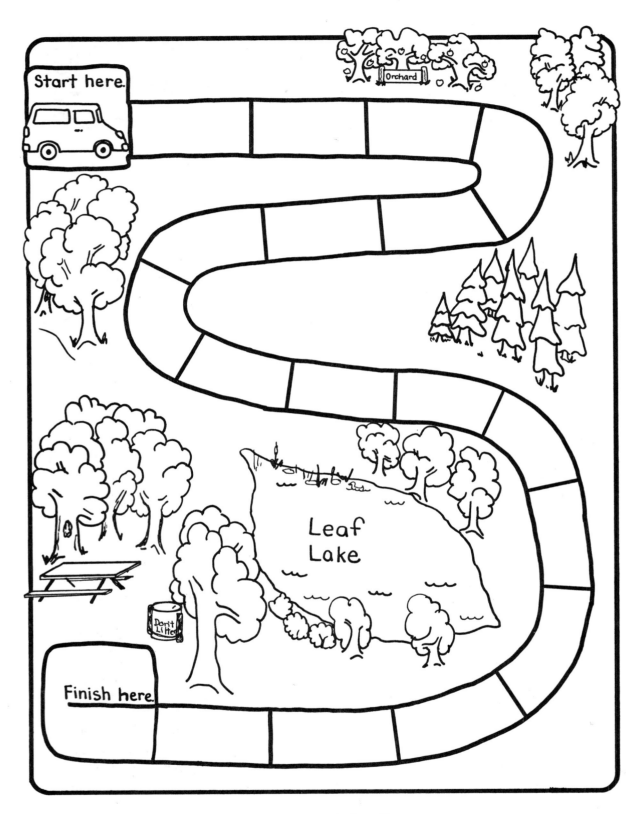

Start here.

Orchard

Leaf Lake

Don't Litter

Finish here.

© 1988 by The Center for Applied Research in Education

Student Activity Page

TEACHER'S DIRECTIONS FOR THE APPLES ACTIVITY

Content areas: Reading, art, science

Skills: Listening, creating, experimenting

Materials needed:

Apples
Paper
Paint: black, red, and green
A piece of sponge approximately 2-by-$\frac{1}{2}$-inches
Two containers such as margarine tubs
Paintbrush
Easel
Old shirt
Tape recorder
Cassette tape
A book about apples such as Anderson, J. I., *I Can Read About Johnny Appleseed,* Troll Associates, Mahwah, N.J., 1977; Bulla, Clyde Robert, *A Tree Is A Plant,* Thomas Y. Crowell Co., New York, 1960.

Materials preparation:

1. Establish background that some trees have edible fruits. Some good books are: Johnson, Hannah Lyons, *From Apple Seed To Applesauce,* Lathrop, Lee and Shepherd Co., New York, 1977; Kohn, Bernice, *Apples . . . A Bushel of Fun and Facts,* Parents' Magazine Press, New York, 1976; Overbeck, Cynthia, *The Fruit Book,* Lerner Publications Co., Minneapolis, 1975; Selsam, Millicent E., *Eat The Fruit, Plant The Seed,* William Morrow and Co., 1980.

2. Prepare the apples for painting. Each day cut one apple in half vertically to show the location of the stem end, the core, and the blossom end. Cut another apple across the core to show the formation of the seed cells in a five pointed star. Put the apple halves in a container. At the end of the day discard the apples and wash the container.

DIRECTIONS FOR FILE FOLDER ACTIVITIES

Activity 1

The student paints an apple tree on paper:

1. He or she uses a paintbrush and black paint to make a tree trunk and branches.
2. The student presses a sponge into a container of green paint then onto the paper to make leaves and grass.
3. The student makes apple prints on the tree. He or she places an apple cut-side down into a container of red paint, then presses it onto the paper. (You may want the student to practice apple printing on newspaper prior to printing on the tree paper.)

Apples

1 Listen to the book.

2 Paint an apple tree.

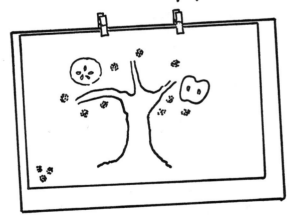

File Folder Directions

TEACHER'S DIRECTIONS FOR THE TREE GROWTH ACTIVITY

Content areas: Science, reading, math, art

Skills: Predicting, communicating, sorting, measuring, observing, classifying, creating, fine-motor coordination, sequencing

Materials needed:

>   Copies of the student activity page
>   Pencil
>   Crayons
>   Teacher-made collection of examples of various growth stages of a tree
>   A container for the tree examples
>   Teacher-made numeral and label cards

Materials preparation:

1. Establish background information for tree growth. Also include knowledge about determining the age of a dead tree by counting the rings. Some books are: Brandt, Keith, *Discovering Trees,* Troll Associates, Mahwah, N.J., 1982; Dowden, Anne Ophelia, *The Blossom On The Bough: A Book Of Trees,* Thomas Y. Crowell Co., New York, 1975; Watson, Aldren A., *A Maple Tree Begins,* Viking Press, New York, 1970.

2. Provide a collection of various examples of growth stages of a tree common to your area. These should include seed, sapling, at least two cross-cut examples of advanced age, and a decaying tree part. Possible sources for the examples may be a tree removal service, lumber mill, local park ranger, or local agriculture agent. If you are unable to obtain these examples of growth stages, pictures or drawings may be substituted. Provide a container for the examples.

3. Use 3-by-5-inch index cards and a water base marking pen to make a set of numeral cards and tree stages cards as pictured on the file folder directions. Laminate the cards and provide a container for them.

DIRECTIONS FOR FILE FOLDER ACTIVITIES

Activity 1

The student sorts and sequences the examples of the tree stages, matching them to numerals and label cards.

Activity 2

The student will draw and compare his or her growth and development to that of a tree on the student activity page.

Tree Growth

1 Sort the tree.
Match the cards.

Tree cards

1	2	3	4	5
seed	sapling	8 years	15 years	rotting wood

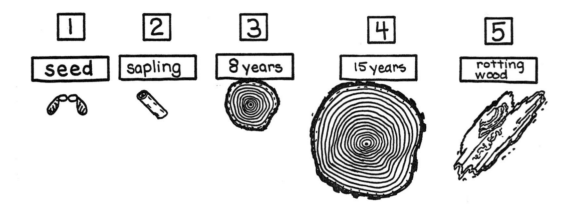

2 Draw a growing tree and yourself.

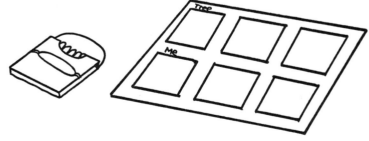

File Folder Directions

A Tree

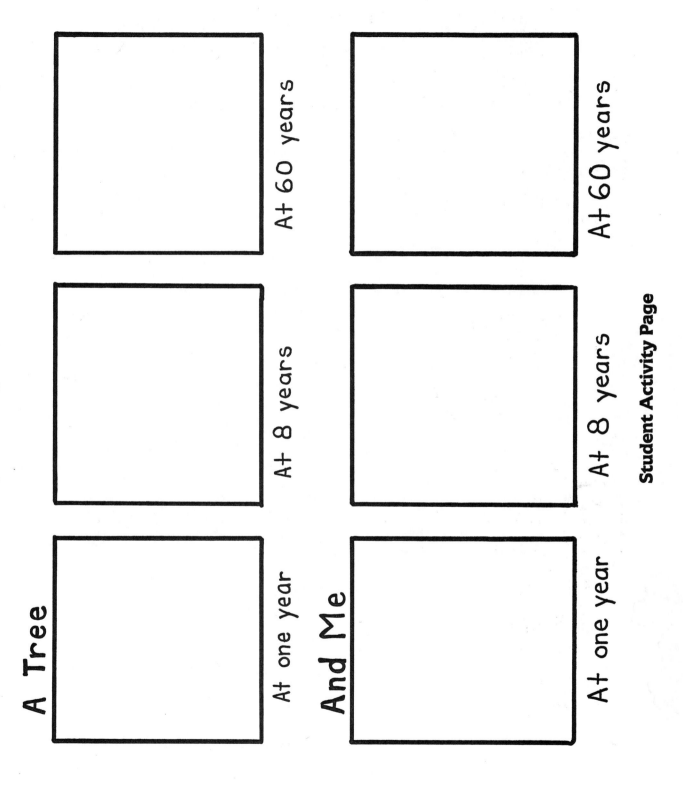

At one year

At 8 years

At 60 years

And Me

At one year

At 8 years

At 60 years

Student Activity Page

TEACHER'S DIRECTIONS FOR THE LEAF CREATURES ACTIVITY

Content areas: Science, art

Skills: Experimenting, creating, communicating, observing, fine-motor coordination, creative writing

Materials needed:

> One piece of 6-by-18-inch yellow, white, or orange construction paper per student
> An assortment of peeled crayons in a variety of colors
> An assortment of fine-tipped water-base marking pens
> A collection of pressed leaves in a catalog
> Magnifying glass

Materials preparation:

1. Provide a collection of pressed leaves in a thick catalog. You may want to take your students on a walk to collect leaves and identify them. Some good books for leaf identification are: Lerner, Sharon, *I Found a Leaf,* Lerner Publications, Minneapolis, 1964; Orange, Anne, *The Leaf Book,* Lerner Publications, Minneapolis, 1975; Petrides, George A., *A Field Guide to Trees and Shrubs,* Houghton Mifflin, Boston, 1973.
2. Encourage the students to look at the leaves with a magnifying glass to observe veins, leaf shapes, and so on.

DIRECTIONS FOR FILE FOLDER ACTIVITIES

Activity 1

The student makes leaf rubbings:

1. The student places one pressed leaf under a strip of construction paper.
2. He or she rubs a crayon over the leaf to create a leaf rubbing.
3. The student continues to follow steps 1 and 2 using a variety of leaves and crayons until he or she has filled the paper with rubbings (approximately five or six leaves).

Activity 2

The student changes the leaf rubbings into creatures. He or she uses marking pens to add paws, hands, heads, feet, clothes, whiskers, glasses, beards, antennas, and so on to the leaf rubbings.

Optional activity

The student can identify leaves using references. He or she can make-up names for his or her creatures and label them. You may want to encourage alliterations such as: "Oak Ogre," "Tulip Tiger," "Maple Martian," "Elm Elephant," "Cottonwood Clown," and so on.

Leaf Creatures

1 Make leaf rubbings.

2 Now make the rubbings into creatures.

Can you name them?

File Folder Directions

Trees
Enrichment Activities

TEACHER'S SUGGESTIONS FOR TREES ENRICHMENT ACTIVITIES

1. Trees Group Activity (refer to p. 181)

Save a Tree Day

2. Trees Home Study (refer to pp. 182–83)

Encourage students to adopt a tree.

3. Trees Award (refer to p. 184)

Ditto the page on colored paper. Give each child who returns the Home Study Adopt a Tree page a Home Study Award. The Trees Award may be used for the recognition of good work, and so on.

4. Trees Evaluation (refer to p. 185)

The evaluations may be stapled to the students tree related work. The grade may be based on a joint teacher-student decision. The student colors in the number of leaves from left to right to indicate his or her performance level. (Left leaf = lowest level, right leaf = highest level).

5. Trees Stump (refer to p. 186)

This page may be used for a "Ways to Save a Tree" story for the group activity or for creative writing. The student begins writing at the "X" on the stump page and continues on the spiral line until he reaches the center of the stump.

6. Trees Bookmark (refer to p. 187)

The student designs three tree bookmarks using real trees or books as references.

7. Trees-Animal Home (refer to p. 188)

The student draws eight animals that might use a tree for their home. He or she may want to use references such as a pictionary or dictionary to make the pictures. The student may want to write a story or list the animals on the back of the page.

GROUP ACTIVITIES

As a culminating activity to the Trees science unit, schedule a "Save a Tree" day. The emphasis would be on recycling. The following are suggested activities that you may want to do:

1. *Recycle Trip.* Plan a walk to collect junk in your area. Divide the students into small groups. Each student will need to carry a used paper bag to collect junk such as leaves, sticks, paper straws, paper wrappers, milk cartons, newspaper, popsicle sticks, and so on. When the students return to the classroom they will work in small groups sorting their junk into tree products and non-tree products. They can make collages or murals using only tree products and appropriate used paper.

2. *Paper bags, magazine, newspaper, and catalog projects.* Throughout the day provide only used paper such as bags, magazines, catalogs, newspaper, and computer paper for all activities. Some ideas are:

    a. Create or copy tree poems from references on pieces of paper bags.

    b. Cut out pictures of tree products from magazines or catalogs and paste them on a paper bag.

    c. Spelling activities: arrange the Spelling list in alphabetical order; take the test or practice words on used computer paper.

    d. Make a list of foods for lunch that could be purchased with $5.00. Use newspaper ads as a reference.

    e. Use a piece of brown paper bag. Draw and cut out a tree with branches. Then circle and cut-out current reading vocabulary words from a newspaper and paste them onto the tree.

3. *Bring items for "Show and Share" that are made out of wood.*

4. *Recycle newspapers.* Collect newspapers if you have a recycling center in your area. Send a letter to parents a month prior to the "Save a Tree" day suggesting that they save newspapers for that day. Recruit parents to arrange a newspaper pick-up from homes if they can not be sent to school on "Save a Tree" day. The same parents may take all of the newspapers to your area's recycling center.

5. *Plant a tree at your school.* You may be able to purchase a tree with any monies gained from the newspaper recycling project. The tree could be cared for and observed throughout the school year.

6. *"Show and Share" the Adopt a Tree Home Study information.*

7. The Enrichment page may be used for an experience story or creative writing.

8. You may want to use the following illustration for parent letters or posters

Trees Home Study
Enrichment Activity Page
Return by _____

Home
Study

Date _____

Dear Parent,

Your child will be studying about trees in our Science unit during the next two weeks.

Please help your child "Adopt a Tree." Take your child to an area such as your yard, neighborhood, or park. Your child may choose a tree that he or she would like to adopt. Help him or her observe and find out the information to complete the attached "Adopt a Tree" paper.

You may want to photograph your child's tree. Your child may want to make a bark rubbing or leaf print of his or her tree. These items may be attached to the "Adopt a Tree" paper and returned on _____.

Encourage your child to continue to observe his or her tree to note changes throughout the year.

Thank you for your help with this project.

Sincerely,

_____
Your child's teacher

Adopt a Tree

(Your child's name) _____

I hugged my tree when I adopted it on _____.
$\qquad\qquad\qquad\qquad\qquad\qquad\qquad\qquad\quad$ *date*

My tree's name is _____.
My tree is an evergreen or deciduous tree (circle one).

My tree is located at _____.

My tree has these parts: _____.

I think my tree is about _____ years old.

My tree is _____ inches around the trunk. I wrapped a piece of string around the trunk, then I measured the string to find out the number of inches.

My tree has had these visitors: _____

_____

My tree is a home for _____.
My tree is special to me because (please use the back of this paper if more space

to write is needed): _____

_____

_____

_____

_____

_____
Parent Signature

Certificate of Adoption

_____

has adopted a tree
by completing the
Home Study Project.

Home Study Award

I cleaned up today.
(I did "mulch" better!)

_____

_____

Trees Award

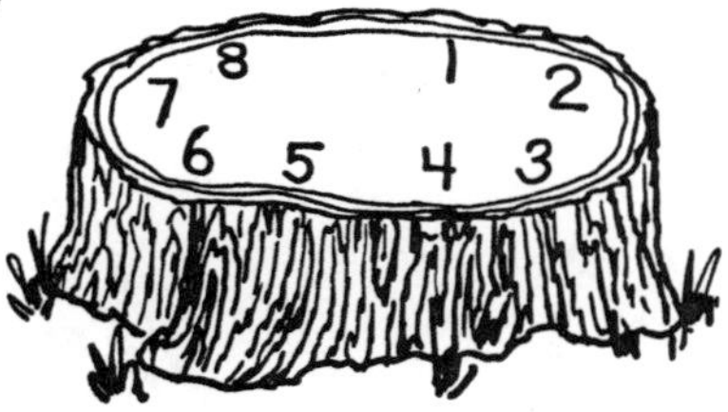

name _____

date _____

I am learning about trees.

My work was _____.

I am learning about trees.

My activity work was _____.

name _____

date _____

Trees Evaluation Page

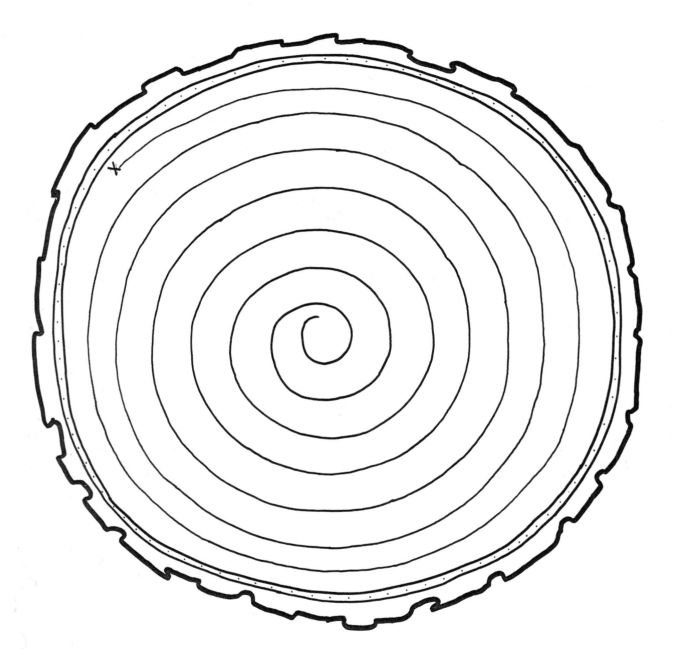

Trees: Stump Enrichment Page

Deciduous	Evergreen	Fruit Tree
_____	_____	_____
name	name	name

Trees: Bookmark Enrichment Page

Draw 8 animals that might use this tree for their home.

_____
name

Trees: Animal Home Enrichment Page

PETS GALORE

Date _____

Dear Parent,

During the next two weeks our science unit will be about pets. Pet care, favorite and unusual pets, animal body coverings, and pets in a shell will be featured.

Your child is welcome to bring a shell collection, puzzles, books, and games. Please be sure that your child's name is on any item brought to class. In addition, please send any shells you would like to donate for the children to share, specify "for sharing."

At the Fish area, your child will make fish flashcards. Hopefully, he or she will want to "fish" for flashcards with another member of your family. A simple fishing pole can be made by tying one end of a string to a ruler and the other end to a magnet.

As one of the art activities, your child will make a diorama of animals that live in shells. Please send an empty shoe box or facial tissue box with your child as soon as possible.

Your child will have an opportunity to use a typewriter to make a pet book. You may want to encourage your child to use a typewriter at home also.

As a group activity we will have two Pet Days. I will send another letter with specific details soon.

Thank you for your continued support.

Sincerely,

_____
Your child's teacher

Pets Center Marker

PETS CENTER MARKER

A learning center marker is provided for students using the science unit activities at learning centers (refer to p. 246).

Distribute copies of the preceding pet store marker to the students. The student draws a pet that he or she has or would like to have on the marker. The students can cut out their markers and place them near the Pet Learning Centers.

PETS ACTIVITIES LIST

These activities emphasize favorite and unusual pets, pet care, pets in a shell, fish, pets in motion, and animal body coverings.

1. **Our Favorite Pets Activity** (a bulletin board is used with this activity)

   Content areas: Science, math

   Skills: Classifying, graphing, fine-motor coordination, communicating, creating

   Activities:

   a. Record favorite pet on a bulletin board.

   b. Make a sewing card of your favorite pet.

2. **Pet Care Activity**

   Content areas: Science, handwriting, art

   Skills: Classifying, sorting, communicating, using reference materials, creating, fine-motor coordination

   Activities:

   a. Sort pet care objects into four containers: Food and Water, Grooming, Exercise, and Shelter.

   b. Record pet care objects' names and pictures on a student activity page.

3. **Pet Book Activity**

   Content areas: Reading, science

   Skills: Fine-motor coordination, alphabetization, using reference materials, communicating

Activities:

  a. Type the alphabet and names of pets on the student activity page.

  b. Illustrate the pet boxes on the student activity page.

  c. Cut apart the pet boxes, arrange them in alphabetical order, and paste them into a Pet Book.

4. Fish Activity (Open-ended activity)

Content areas: Math, teacher's choice

Skills: Fine-motor coordination, teacher's choice, using reference materials, communicating

Activities:

  a. Make a fishing game using the student activity page.

  b. Play the fishing game alone or with a friend.

5. Pets in Motion Activity

Content areas: Science, art, handwriting

Skills: Classifying, creating, communicating, using reference materials, fine-motor coordination

Activities:

  a. Label three columns on handwriting paper: swim, fly, and crawl or walk.

  b. Write pet names in each category using references.

  c. Use construction paper to make pets that swim, fly, and crawl or walk for a mural.

6. Animal Body Coverings Activity

Content areas: Science, reading, handwriting

Skills: Sorting, classifying, observing, communicating, creating, creative writing

Activities:

  a. Observe and sort a collection of animal coverings.

  b. Write and illustrate an animal riddle on the student activity page.

7. Pets in Shells Activity

Content areas: Science, reading, art

Skills: Listening, sorting, classifying, creating, observing, experimenting

Activities:

a. Listen to the story about animals in a shell.
b. Sort a collection of shells into containers.
c. Make a diorama.

8. Unusual Pets Activity

Content areas: Handwriting, art, reading

Skills: Creative writing, creating, using reference materials, communicating, fine-motor coordination

Activities:

a. Write a story about an unusual pet using references.
b. Paint a picture of the unusual pet.

TEACHER'S DIRECTIONS FOR OUR FAVORITE PETS ACTIVITY

Content areas: Science, math

Skills: Classifying, graphing, communicating, fine-motor coordination, creating

Materials needed:

  Bulletin board
  One 3-by-5-inch index card per student
  Thumbtacks and container
  Pencil
  Crayons
  Paper puncher
  One 8½-by-11-inch piece of oaktag per student
  Scissors
  Yarn
  Bobby pin
  Teacher-made sewing card patterns

Materials preparation:

1. Make "Our Favorite Pets" bulletin board as shown on the file folder directions page.
2. Make four sewing card patterns on oaktag (refer to upcoming teacher directions pages). Laminate the patterns, then punch holes with a paper puncher.
   Optional: Older students may wish to design their own sewing card without a pattern.

DIRECTIONS FOR FILE FOLDER ACTIVITIES

Activity 1

1. The student writes his or her name on an index card.
2. The student tacks his or her card next to his or her favorite pet choice.

Activity 2

1. The student traces one of the pet patterns of his or her choice on oaktag.
2. He or she colors, cuts, and punches holes to make a sewing card.
3. The student uses a piece of yarn threaded through a bobby pin to sew the card.

Our Favorite Pets

© 1988 by The Center for Applied Research in Education

1

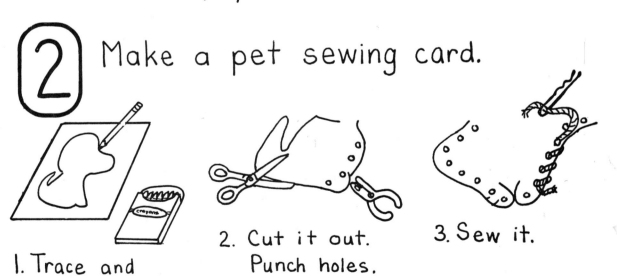

Our Favorite Pets

Pets:

cat	Jason Alan
fish	Adam
dog	Jon Sarah Craig Ethan
bird	Amy Jason Cari

Number of students: 1 2 3 4 5 6 7 8 9 10 11 12 13 14 15

Put your name on a card.
Tack it by your favorite pet.

2 Make a pet sewing card.

1. Trace and color it.

2. Cut it out. Punch holes.

3. Sew it.

File Folder Directions

Teacher Directions Page

Teacher Directions Page

Teacher Directions Page

Teacher Directions Page

TEACHER'S DIRECTIONS FOR THE PET CARE ACTIVITY

Content areas: Science, handwriting, art

Skills: Classifying, sorting, communicating, using reference materials, creating, fine-motor coordination

Materials needed:

An assortment of objects or pictures for the following pet care needs:

1. Food and water: dog food, bone, cat food, seed bell, fish food, hamster food, carrot, lettuce fruit, bowl, fountain feeder, and drinking tube.
2. Grooming: nail clippers, toothbrush, comb, brush, file, cuttlebone, grit, shampoo, soap, flea and tick powder.
3. Exercise: ball, bell, ball of yarn, play hoops, leash, collar, mirror, ferris wheel (parakeets), castle (fish), wheel (gerbils and hamsters), and paper tubes.
4. Shelter: aquarium, dog house, basket, cage, barn, blanket, litter, wood chips, marble chips, newspaper.

Box for the objects
Four containers such as boxes, carpet samples, place mats
Copies of student activity page
Pencil
Crayons

Materials preparation:

1. Write the word on each pet care object.
2. Label the four containers: Food and Water, Grooming, Exercise, Shelter.
3. Discuss pet care with your students. Be sure they understand that pets need food, water, grooming, exercise, and shelter to stay healthy. Explain the Pet Care activity will be about the pet they have or the animal they would like to have for a pet.
4. Make an example student activity page, fold on the dotted line, write "My Pet _____" at the top of the page, leave the remaining space empty for the student to draw a picture of his or her pet.

DIRECTIONS FOR FILE FOLDER ACTIVITIES

Activity 1

The student sorts the pet care objects into the four containers: Food and Water, Grooming, Exercise, and Shelter.

Activity 2

1. The student draws and labels the objects his or her pet would need in each category on the student activity page.
2. He or she refers to your example to fold, write, and draw his or her pet.

Optional activity

The older student may write a story about his or her pet or the animal he or she would like to have for a pet. He or she may want to include pet selection, name selection, pet care jobs he or she likes or dislikes, and so on.

Pet Care

1 Pet Care

food and water grooming

exercise shelter

Sort the objects.

2 Do the ditto about a pet.

Draw the pet on the front. ↓

Pet Pet Needs

File Folder Directions

Pet Needs:

Food and Water

Grooming

Exercise

Shelter

...and Love!

_____
name

Food and Water	Grooming
Exercise	Shelter

Student Activity Page

TEACHER'S DIRECTIONS FOR THE PET BOOK ACTIVITY

Content areas: Reading, science

Skills: Fine-motor coordination, alphabetization, using reference materials, communicating

Materials needed:

> Copies of student activity page
> Old typewriter
> Crayons
> Scissors
> Paste
> Pencil
> References: pictionary, dictionary, animal books, animal charts
> Blank books consisting of three folded sheets of paper per book as shown here

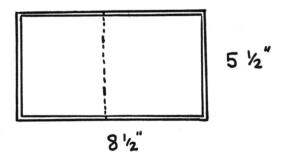

Materials preparation:

1. Instruct the students on the proper way to load the student activity page into the typewriter carriage. If this is the students' first experience with classroom typing, assure the students that mistakes will be acceptable.
2. Encourage the students to proofread their typing *after* the paper is removed from the typewriter. They may use a pencil to cross out any errors or write in missing letters (no erasing is allowed).
3. If a typewriter is not available, these options may work: 1. write words in each box; 2. use a stamp letter set and ink pad to print the letters; 3. use a computer and printer if the students have adequate skills.

DIRECTIONS FOR FILE FOLDER ACTIVITIES

Activity 1

1. The student types the alphabet as a reference for alphabetical order on the student activity page.
2. He or she types the name of the pet at the bottom of each box on the student activity page.
3. He or she illustrates the boxes, referring to a pictionary, dictionary, or chart.

Activity 2

1. The student cuts the pet boxes apart and arranges them in alphabetical order.
2. He or she pastes the boxes into the blank books in alphabetical order.
3. The student writes "My Pet Book" and his or her name on the cover.
4. An older student may be encouraged to write a sentence about each animal, such as, "A dog lives in _____." "It eats _____."

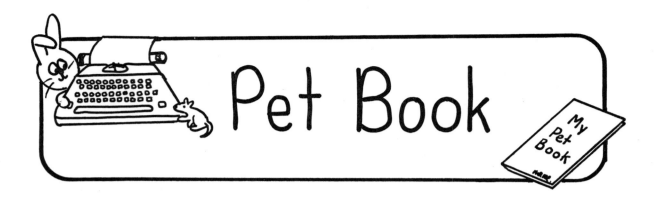

Pet Book

1 Type the abc's.
Type names of pets.

Now draw the pets.

2 Cut apart the pictures.
Put in abc order.

Paste them into a book.

File Folder Directions

Pets

Type the abc's here.

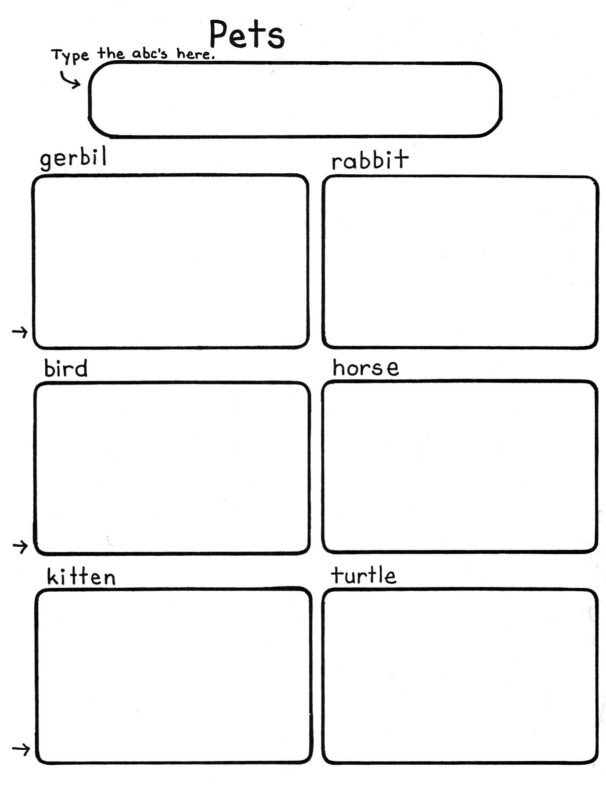

gerbil

rabbit

bird

horse

kitten

turtle

Student Activity Page

TEACHER'S DIRECTIONS FOR THE FISH ACTIVITY

Content areas: Math, teacher's choice (refer to p. **x**)

Skills: Fine-motor coordination, teacher's choice, using reference materials, communicating

Materials needed:

> Copies of student activity page (ditto on construction paper)
> Stapler and staples
> Meter stick, ruler, or dowel
> String approximately three feet long
> Magnet
> Scissors
> Pencil
> One envelope per student
> Teacher-made reference chart

Materials preparation:

1. To make the reference chart, use a copy of the student activity page to reinforce or review a skill, such as math problems or numerals/names of numerals.
2. Make a fishing pole by attaching one end of the string to a meter stick and the opposite end to a magnet.
3. *Optional:* You may want to display books, pictures, or charts of fish common to your area. The student may want to color his or her fish on the student activity page similar to a specific kind. Fish charts may be available through the U. S. Department of Interior, Fish and Wildlife Service, Washington, D. C. 20240; National Wildlife Federation, 1412 16th St., N.W., Washington, D. C. 20036-2266; your state Department of Natural Resources or Conservation.

DIRECTIONS FOR FILE FOLDER ACTIVITIES

Activity 1

1. The student copies the reference chart on a student activity page, then completes the work. For example, when solving math problems, the student could write the answers on the back of the fish.
2. The student cuts out the fish.
3. He or she uses the stapler to put two staples in the form of an X on each fish.

Activity 2

1. The student lays the fish on the floor.
2. He or she may play the fishing game alone or with a friend.
3. The student puts the fish in an envelope.

Fish

1 Make a fish game.

Write.   Cut.   Staple X.

2 Play your game
with a friend.

File Folder Directions

Student Activity Page

TEACHER'S DIRECTIONS FOR THE PETS IN MOTION ACTIVITY

Content areas: Science, art, handwriting

Skills: Classifying, creating, communicating, using reference materials, fine-motor coordination

Materials needed:

> Handwriting paper
> Pencil
> Crayons
> Scissors
> Paste
> Construction paper in assorted sizes and colors
> References: animal books, dictionary, pictionary, encyclopedias

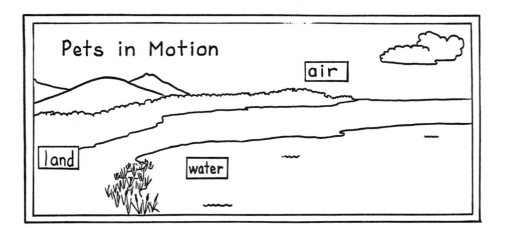

Materials preparation:

1. Prepare an area such as a bulletin board, floor, table, for a "Pets in Motion" mural as shown here
2. Be sure the students understand that pets live in the air, on land, and in water. Encourage the students to make a variety of pets for the mural to prevent duplication of common ones. Emphasize that insects, as well as birds, can fly.
3. *Optional:* Display several small animals such as worms, fish, and insects for the students to observe.

DIRECTIONS FOR FILE FOLDER ACTIVITIES

Activity 1

The student folds handwriting paper into three columns. He or she labels the columns, "swim," "fly," and "crawl or walk." The student writes pet names in each category using references. You determine the number required for each category.

Activity 2

The student uses crayons, scissors, and construction paper to make pets that swim, fly, and crawl or walk. He or she pastes the pets onto the mural. You determine the number required for each category.

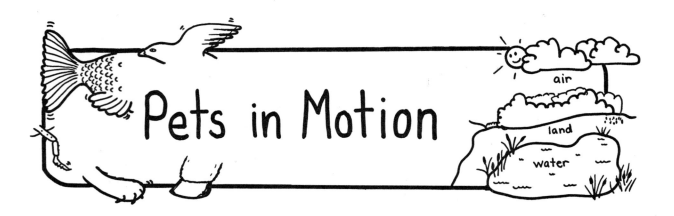

Pets in Motion

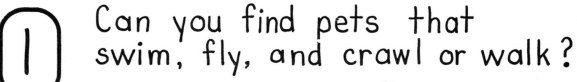
Can you find pets that swim, fly, and crawl or walk?

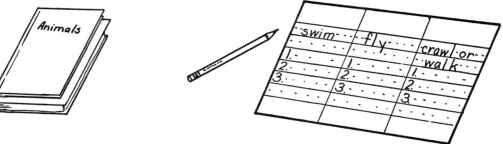

Make pets that can swim, fly, and crawl or walk.

File Folder Directions

TEACHER'S DIRECTIONS FOR THE ANIMAL BODY COVERINGS ACTIVITY

Content areas: Science, reading, handwriting

Skills: Sorting, classifying, observing, communicating, creating, creative writing

Materials needed:

> Copies of student activity page
> Pencil
> Crayons
> Magnifying glass
> Teacher-made collection of animal body covering samples or pictures
> Four containers

Materials preparation:

1. Prepare a collection of animal body covering samples or pictures including, feathers, scales, shells, and fur. Label a container for each category.
2. Discuss the functions of various animal's body coverings such as protection, coloration, insulation from weather conditions, and so on.
3. Be sure the students understand riddles.
4. *Optional:* Display small animals with each body covering category for the students to observe.

DIRECTIONS FOR FILE FOLDER ACTIVITIES

Activity 1

The student looks at the collection of animal body coverings. He or she may use a magnifying glass.

Activity 2

The student sorts the collection of animal coverings into the four containers; feathers, scales, shells, and fur.

Activity 3

The student writes and illustrates an animal riddle on the student activity page. You determine the required number of riddles.

Optional activity

The students may share their riddles with the class or another class at a prearranged time that day.

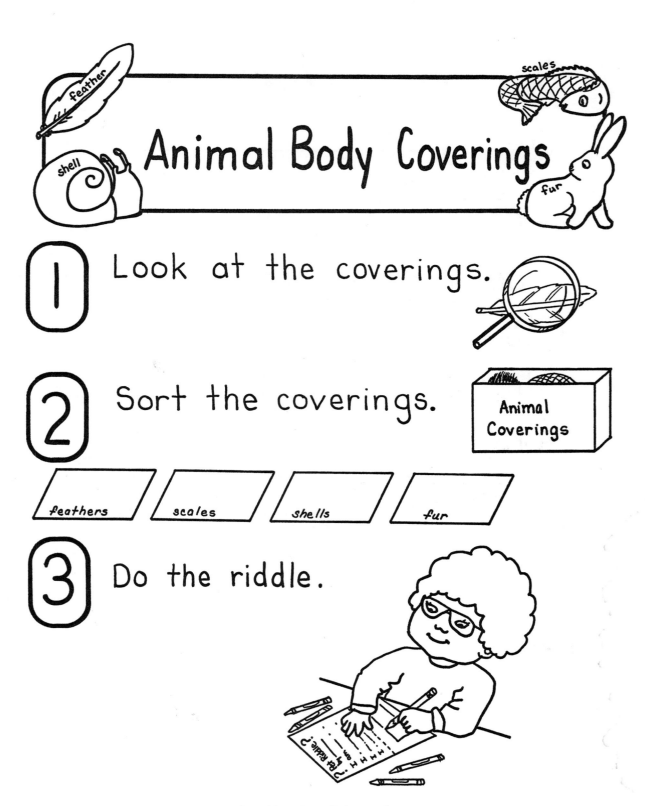

Animal Body Coverings

1 Look at the coverings.

2 Sort the coverings.

Animal Coverings

feathers | scales | shells | fur

3 Do the riddle.

File Folder Directions

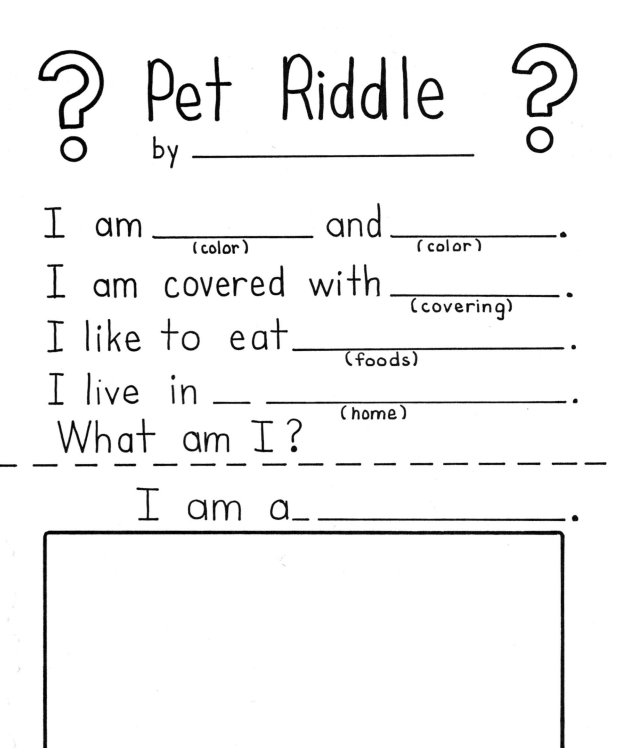

? Pet Riddle ?

by _____

I am _____ and _____.
       (color)   (color)

I am covered with _____.
                 (covering)

I like to eat_____.
          (foods)

I live in __ _____.
         (home)

What am I?

- - - - - - - - - - - - - - - - - - - -

I am a_____.

↑ Fold up to dashed line. ↑

Student Activity Page

TEACHER'S DIRECTIONS FOR THE PETS IN SHELLS ACTIVITY

Content areas: Science, reading, art

Skills: Listening, sorting, classifying, creating, observing, experimenting

Materials needed:

A collection of shells such as auger, clam, cockle, conch, cowrie, periwinkle, scallop, and whelk.

Containers for shells, such as egg cartons

One shoe box or facial tissue box per student

Clay

Container and lid for clay

Marking pens in dark colors

An assortment of scrap materials such as pipe cleaners, yarn, construction paper, sequins

Scissors

Paste

Tape recorder

Cassette tape

A book about animals in shells such as Blough, Glenn O. and Bendick, Jeanne, *Who Lives at the Seashore?*, McGraw-Hill, New York, 1962; Goudey, Alice E., *Houses from the Sea*, Charles Scribner's Sons, New York, 1959; Lubell, Winifred and Cecil, *By the Seashore*, Parent's Magazine Press, New York, 1975; Selsam, Millicent E., *Animals of the Sea*, Scholastic, Inc., New York, 1975.

Materials preparation:

1. Tape record the book you have chosen for this activity.
2. You may want to make an example diorama.
3. *Optional:* Display a live hermit crab, snail, clam, or other animal that lives in a shell in an appropriate container for the students to observe.

DIRECTIONS FOR FILE FOLDER ACTIVITIES

Activity 1

The student listens to the story.

Activity 2

The student sorts the shells into containers. You may want to label the containers "Large and Small," "Spirals and Not Spirals," "Univalves and Bivalves," and so on.

Activity 3

The student creates a diorama:

1. The student uses marking pens to make the background of water and land inside the shoe box.
2. He or she uses an assortment of scrap materials to make plant pictures. He pastes the plants to the bottom and sides of the shoe box.
3. The student chooses one or more shells from the shell collection.
4. He or she uses clay and scrap materials to create an animal in each shell for the diorama.

Pets in Shells

1. Listen to the book.

2. Sort the shells.

3. Make a diorama.

Make animals for it.

File Folder Directions

TEACHER'S DIRECTIONS FOR THE UNUSUAL PETS ACTIVITY

Content areas: Handwriting, art, reading

Skills: Creative writing, creating, using reference materials, communicating, fine-motor coordination

Materials needed:

> Paint
> Paintbrushes
> Easel
> Paper
> Pencil
> References: pictionary, dictionary, encyclopedias, pet books such as Hess, Lilo, *Problem Pets,* Charles Scribner's Sons, New York, 1972; Kaufman, Elizabeth Elias, *Pets,* Price/Stern/Sloan Publishers Inc., Los Angeles, 1986; Simon, Seymour, *Pets in a Jar,* The Viking Press Inc., New York, 1975; Stein, Sara, *Great Pets!,* Workman Publishing Co. Inc., New York, 1976.

Materials preparation:

> Display several pet books. In addition, you may want to use audiovisual aids to establish background information about unusual pets.

DIRECTIONS FOR FILE FOLDER ACTIVITIES

Activity 1

> The student writes a story about an unusual pet using the available references.

Activity 2

> The student paints a picture of the unusual pet.

Unusual Pets

1 Write about an unusual pet.

2 Paint a picture of the unusual pet.

File Folder Directions

Pet
Enrichment Activities

Unit 5
PETS

Pet Shop

OPEN

We ♡ Pets!

TEACHER'S SUGGESTIONS FOR PET ENRICHMENT ACTIVITIES

1. **Pet Group Activities** (refer to pp. 228-29)

    Pet Days

2. **Pet Home Study** (refer to p. 230)

    Encourage parents to take their child to visit a pet store, zoo, farm, or veterinarian to find out information about pets.

3. **Pets Award** (refer to p. 231)

    Ditto the page on colored paper. Give each child who returns the Home Study note a Home Study Award. The Pet Award may be used for the recognition of good work, and so on.

4. **Pets Evaluation** (refer to p. 232)

    The evaluations may be stapled daily to the student's pet related work. The grade may be based on a joint teacher-student decision. The student colors in the appropriate number of tracks from the house to indicate his or her performance level. (The track nearest the dog house is the lowest level with the track nearest the bone the highest level.)

5. **Pets Cage** (refer to p. 233)

    This page may be used for the cover of an experience story following the Pet Days group activity or for creative writing. Prior to writing the story the student will lay the student activity page on top of handwriting paper. He or she will cut the papers simultaneously. The student will write the story on the handwriting paper. Then he or she will illustrate the animal he wrote about in the Cage student activity page. The cage page may be stapled onto the handwriting paper for a cover. Some creative writing ideas are "A funny thing happened with _____." "I liked _____'s pet because _____." "The pet that did funny tricks was _____."

6. Lost Pet (refer to p. 234)

The student will draw a picture of a lost pet and write a "lost pet" ad for a newspaper listing what type of pet was lost, the pet's name, what color and size it was, when it was lost, where it was lost, reward offered, whom to return it to, address, and telephone number. You may want to make a reference chart or information form for the student to copy.

7. Pet Bathtub (refer to p. 235)

This page may be used for creative writing. The student writes a story about how a pet keeps clean referring to the vocabulary listed. The student may illustrate the story on the back of the page. You may want to discuss pet cleanliness habits prior to using this page.

GROUP ACTIVITIES

As a culminating activity to the Pets science unit, schedule two pet days. Send the following letter to parents at least one week before the events.

Prior to pet days, a class discussion should be held about bringing pets and pet food in proper containers. If the pets are unable to come to school, suggest that photographs be brought on pet days. Encourage the students who do not have pets to bring a favorite stuffed animal.

During the two pet days, the student should have the opportunity to tell about his or her pet, pet photograph, or stuffed animal. He or she should also answer any questions regarding his or her pet.

If possible, plan to take your students to a prearranged outside area when cats and dogs come to visit. It works well to have the students sit in a large circle on the ground. The student with his cat or dog can take a turn standing in the center of the circle. He or she may tell about his or her pet and answer questions about it.

Follow-up Activity

The Pet Bathtub enrichment page may be used for an experience story or creative writing on pet days.

PET DAYS

Date _____

Dear Parent,

Many children have wanted to bring their pets to school this year. As a culminating activity to our Pets science unit we will have two pet days. Pets may come at the following times:

Small pets in proper containers may spend the day at school on
_____ or _____.
Dogs accompanied by an adult are welcome to visit on
_____ at _____.
Cats accompanied by an adult are welcome to visit on
_____ at _____.

Photographs of pets may be sent to school on pet days if it is inconvenient to bring pets. If your child does not have a pet, he or she may bring in a favorite stuffed animal.

I am looking forward to seeing you soon. Feel free to come on any pet day or anytime between the hours of _____and _____to see our pet unit activities.

Thank you for your continued support.

Sincerely,

_____
Your child's teacher

Pet Home Study
Enrichment Activity Page
Return by _____

Date _____

Dear Parent,

Your child will be studying about pets during the next two weeks.

Please take your child to visit a pet store, zoo, farm, or veterinarian. If it is impossible, perhaps a telephone call could be arranged to one of them. Please help your child find out the following information:

1. What kind of animal would make a good pet for your family?
2. What type of care would the pet require?
3. How much would the pet's food cost for one week?
4. What kind of home would the pet need?
5. Would the pet need to go to a veterinarian? How often?

Please return the following note by _____. Thank you for your continued support.

Sincerely,

_____
Your child's teacher

- -

Pet Home Study

_____
Your child's name

I visited _____ on _____.
　　　　　　　place　　　　　　　　　　*date*

I learned about _____.
　　　　　　　animal's name

_____
Parent's signature

Pet Detective

I learned about pets at the _____.

_____
name

Home Study Award

Great Going !

_____
_____
_____
_____

Pets Award

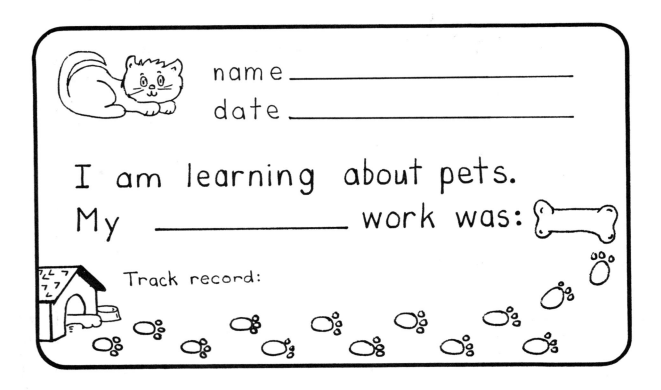

name _____

date _____

I am learning about pets.

My _____ work was:

Track record: _____

name _____

date _____

I am learning about pets.

Today I worked on the

_____ activity.

My work was:

Pets Evaluation Page

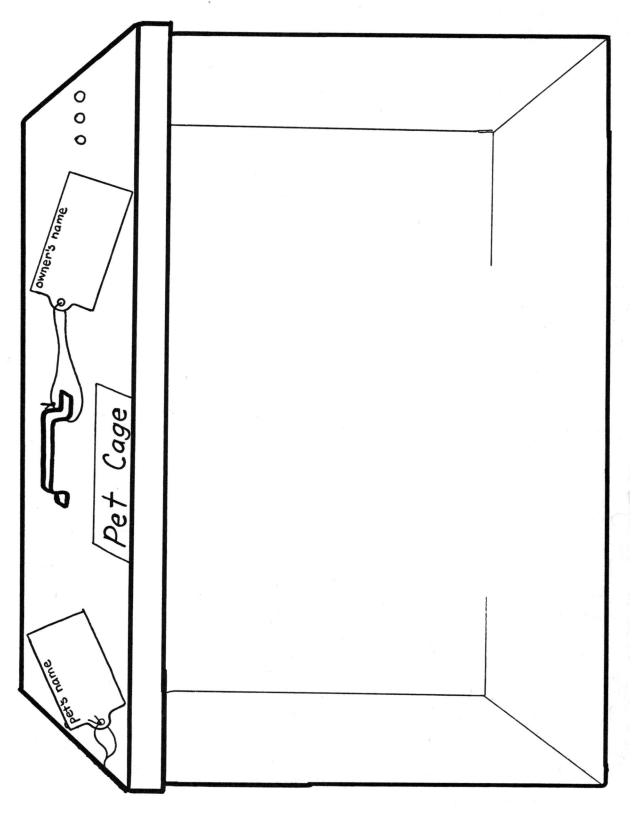

Pets: Cage Enrichment Page

Lost:
my pet_____

_____
_____
_____
_____
_____
_____
_____
_____
_____
_____
_____

Pet Owner:_____

Pets: Lost Pet Enrichment Page

How do pets keep clean?

Name

Word Bank:

bath	shower		
mud	roll		
water	paws		
claw	soap		

swim	splash	tongue	dust
feathers	wash	shake	insects
lick	dry	preen	wet
shampoo	fleas	towel	brush
		feet	scratch

ears	dirt
tail	comb
powder	

Pets: Bathtub Enrichment Page

MANAGEMENT
UNIT

LEARNING CENTER BIBLIOGRAPHY

The science unit activities may be used at Learning Centers. If you want to begin using Learning Centers, but need management techniques, you may want to try a management system that has worked successfully for us. A brief synopsis of this system is given in this chapter. More specific details of this system are described extensively in the following book: Poppe, Carol A. and Van Matre, Nancy A., *Science Learning Centers for the Primary Grades,* The Center for Applied Research in Education, Inc., West Nyack, New York, 1985.

Additional Learning Center ideas are given in the following books:

Borba, Craig, and Borba, Michele, *The Good Apple Guide to Learning Centers,* Good Apple, Inc., Carthage, IL, 1978.

Davidson, Tom, and Steely, Judy, *Using Learning Centers with Not-Yet Readers.* Goodyear Publishing Co., Santa Monica, CA, 1978.

Kaplan, Sandra N. and Jo Ann B., Madsen, Sheila K., and Gould, Bette Taylor, *A Young Child Experiences,* Pacific Palisades, CA: Goodyear Publishing Co., 1975.

Lorton, Mary B., *Work Jobs,* Addison-Wesley Publishing Co., Menlo Park, CA, 1972.

How to Manage a Learning Center System

This system features Learning Center Unit activities as an integral part of a daily schedule.

The children are taught in a traditional manner for the initial three weeks of the school year. All of the children are assigned morning seatwork. You work with small groups of children to assess their reading ability.

You establish four reading groups based on ability. Each group is given a color name: red, yellow, orange, and green.

After the four groups are established the children are introduced to a new morning routine. (See the following sample morning schedule.) The children move every one half hour to four areas of the classroom to do seatwork, boardwork, reading, and learning center activities (one child per Learning Center).

A color wheel displayed near the reading area aids in the clockwise movement of the four groups to the four areas of the room.

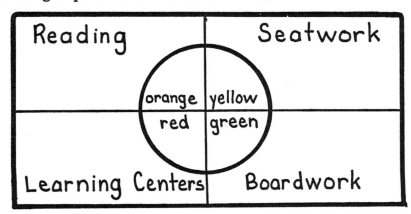

You turn the color wheel clockwise after you have completed one half hour with a reading group. The groups rotate until they have completed the four areas (approximately two hours every morning).

A "makeup" time of approximately fifteen minutes is held after all four reading groups are finished. Children with incomplete work (which has been placed in a box labeled "Makeup") have the opportunity to complete their work. The other children use this time for games, books, and so on.

The afternoon schedule consists of whole group activities: math, writing, gym, social studies, art, phonics, and so on.

Morning Schedule

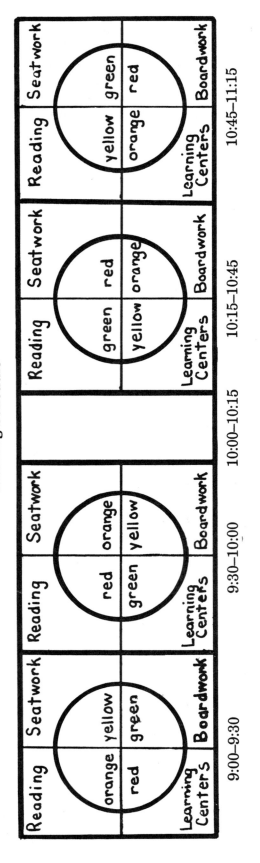

8:30–9:00	Group	9:00–9:30	9:30–10:00	10:00–10:15	10:15–10:45	10:45–11:15	11:15–11:30
Whole class is at Seat- work and Boardwork desks for Opening and Seatwork, Boardwork Directions	orange	Reading	Seatwork	Recess	Boardwork	Learning Centers	Makeup
	yellow	Seatwork	Boardwork	Recess	Learning Centers	Reading	Makeup
	red	Learning Centers	Reading	Recess	Seatwork	Boardwork	Makeup
	green	Boardwork	Learning Centers	Recess	Reading	Seatwork	Makeup

Alternative Group Suggestions

1. If you switch students for reading instruction, you could group them according to math ability.

2. You could have four groups of children going to five learning centers (two children per learning center in each group). Learning centers would then be changed at the end of five days.

3. You may prefer to have five groups moving to five room areas for reading, phonics (reading workbooks), math, boardwork, and learning centers. The activities could last thirty minutes.

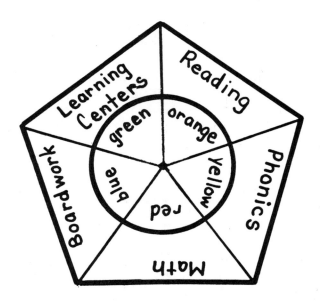

How to Make a Color Wheel

You will need the following materials:

One piece of 14-by-22-inch blue posterboard
One circular piece of white posterboard 7 inches in diameter
One brass fastener 1/2 inch long
One black, red, yellow, orange, and green marking pen
One yardstick

Use the yardstick and the black marking pen to divide the blue poster-board into fourths. Write each of the four room areas (reading, seatwork, learning centers, and boardwork) in a different section of the posterboard. Use the yard-stick and black marking pen again to divide the circular piece of posterboard into fourths. Color one-fourth of the circular piece red, one-fourth yellow, one-fourth green, and one-fourth orange. (The color arrangement depends on the order in which you want the four groups to move to the four areas.) Use the brass fastener to connect the center of the Color Wheel to the center of the blue posterboard.

How to Set up the Classroom into Four Areas: Seatwork, Boardwork, Reading, and Learning Centers:

The arrangement of the furniture in the classroom is important in creating a good learning environment. The room should be set up to give the students the freedom to move physically and academically from one area to another.

Prior to the first day of school, arrange the furniture to create four areas: seatwork, boardwork, reading, and learning centers. It is easier to develop a set routine in the beginning weeks of the school year than to rearrange the classroom when you start the four group movement (approximately a month later).

The main area of the classroom should be divided into two parts: one for seatwork and one for boardwork. Bookcases, storage boxes, and so on can be placed in a long row to serve as a main divider between the seatwork and boardwork areas. (See the following diagram.)

The desks in the boardwork area will usually face a chalkboard. The students will be copying your assignments from the chalkboard. Some ideas are the Enrichment Activities given in each science unit chapter: creative writing, riddles, and so on.

In the seatwork area, the desks do not need to face the chalkboard. Seatwork activities may include: phonics, spelling, mathematics, social studies, and reading ditto or workbook pages. Many of the Enrichment Activities given in each science unit chapter are also suitable for seatwork.

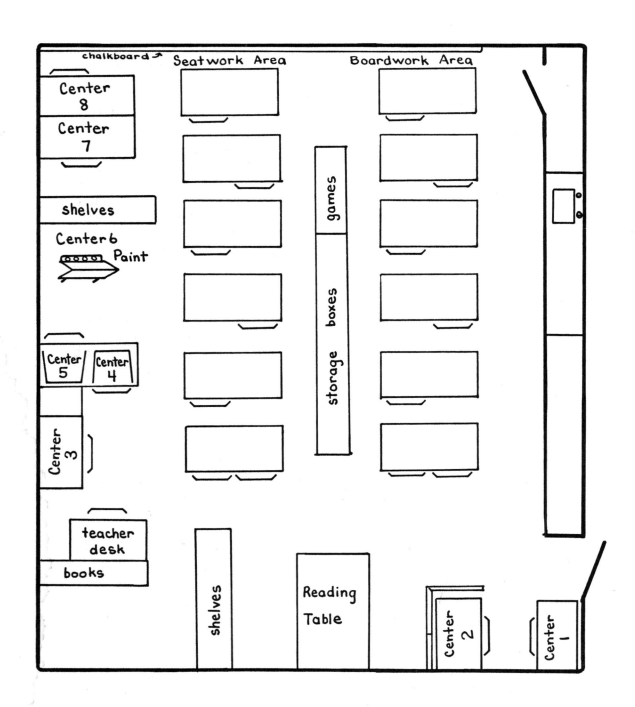

How to Assign Desks

An important factor to consider in room arrangement is the assignment of desks. Each child can have a permanently assigned desk to use before school and during the whole-group activities of the day. In order to accommodate the mobility of the four groups to seatwork, boardwork, learning centers, and reading, all of the desk tops can be shared by everyone. (You may need to establish a rule that everyone works on desk tops only.)

Supplies such as pencils, crayons, scissors, and paste can be kept at a central location (countertop, three-tiered cart, or bookcase, for example). The children can use these supplies during seatwork, boardwork, and learning centers. You may want each child to have a small box of supplies in his or her own desk so that the child can carry the box to the various work areas of the room.

There is an alternative method for seating that allows for maximum mobility in the classroom. The children do not have any assigned desks; only the tops of the desks are used, not the insides. (You may prefer to turn the desks so the open ends are away from the seated children.)

Each child needs a shoe box or something similar for his or her supplies. The shoe boxes are stored on a bookshelf that is easily accessible to the children. When a child enters the room each morning, he or she puts the shoe box on an empty seatwork or boardwork desk. The child uses this desk before school and during whole-group activities. When the child moves with his or her group to learning centers, seatwork, boardwork he or she brings the shoe box. During reading, the shoe box is put on the bookshelf.

How to Keep Track of Each Child at Learning Centers

Ditto a center marker for each child as pictured on p. 246. Write the child's name on the marker (after it has been run on the ditto machine).

Sort the markers into the four groups (red, orange, yellow, and green). Circle a different number on each child's marker in the red group with a permanent marking pen. (In this way, each child in the red group starts at a different learning center.) Circle the numbers on the markers for the orange, yellow, and green groups in the same way.

Pass out the markers to each child to color and cut out. (It is helpful to have each child color his marker the color of his group, especially with the initial set of learning centers.)

After the children have colored and cut out their markers, staple them on a bulletin board or divider into four groups. The markers should be near the reading area since the children move there after they finish learning centers.

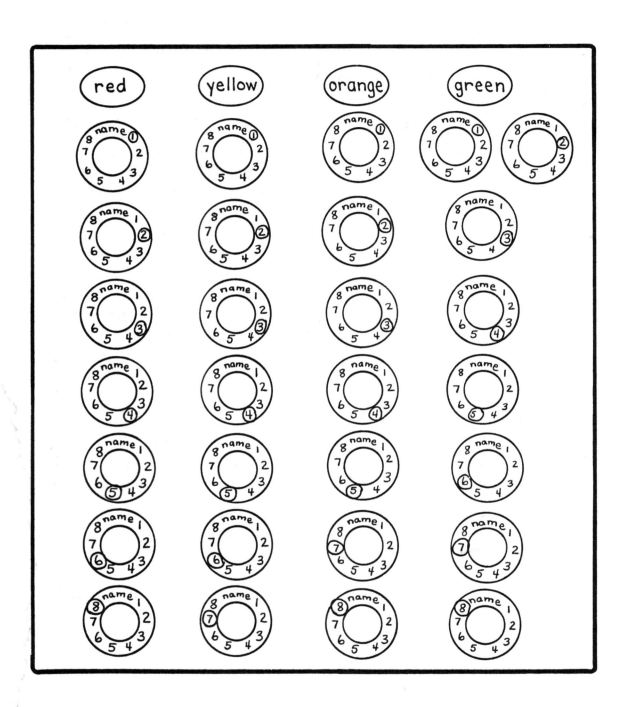

When the child has finished his learning center, he moves with his group to the reading area. He finds his marker on the bulletin board. Using a permanent marking pen, he puts an "X" on the number of the learning center he finished. Then he circles the next number in clockwise order. This is the number of the learning center where he will work the following day. He continues this pattern daily until he has completed all learning centers (one per day). In the example pictured below, he would do a total of eight learning centers during an eight day period.

　　　　If a child is absent, the teacher marks "Ab." next to the number of that child's learning center. Then the teacher circles the following day's center number. The learning centers missed due to absences are *not* made up. This is essential in keeping one child per learning center.

How to Evaluate the Learning Center Activities

When a group of students rotates to the reading area they bring their completed learning centers work to be graded.

There are a variety of evaluation techniques. One method you may wish to use enables both the student and the teacher to give input into the evaluation. Quality of work, following directions, ways to improve, and so on are discussed. The evaluation is based on a joint student-teacher decision.

The Enrichment Activities of each science unit contain evaluation forms. The forms may be used daily to measure the student's progress. They may be attached to a student's learning center work.

How to Introduce a New Set of Learning Centers to the Entire Class

1. Seat all of the children on the floor near the first learning center. (After you have finished the directions for the first learning center, the group continues to move with you to each additional learning center. This may take thirty to forty-five minutes to explain eight learning centers. No additional directions will be necessary for the eight day period.)

2. Explain the directions in consecutive order at each learning center.

3. Demonstrate any special equipment (e.g., filmstrip pre-viewer) at the learning center.

4. Discuss the proper care of materials (e.g., shells or fragile items). If materials were borrowed from a media center, you may wish to emphasize special handling.

5. Indicate any activities that need to be checked by you before the child leaves the learning center (e.g., manipulatives on a bulletin board or flannelboard or floor activities). Work out a signal for the child so you don't forget to check his work (e.g., child can remain standing at the learning center with two arms raised).

6. Discuss clean-up rules. If the learning center is disorderly when a child goes to it, he should get the child who preceded him to clean up.

7. Allow time for questions at each learning center. By explaining a set of learning centers thoroughly, you will eliminate daily interruptions. A child may quietly ask another person in his group for additional help with directions.

How to Explain Learning Centers to Parents

The following letter is sent home on the first day that learning centers are used (approximately the third week of September).

ALL ABOUT LEARNING CENTERS

Date _____

Dear Parent:

During the first few weeks of school, I have been reviewing the skills your child has learned in the past. The children have been given a variety of tests.

Today we began a new morning routine that we will follow all year. The children have been divided into four groups based on reading ability. The four groups are: red, green, yellow, and orange. The children move every one-half hour to four areas of the classroom to do seatwork, boardwork, reading, and learning center activities.

A color wheel (in the center of this diagram) helps all of us keep track of where we are working:

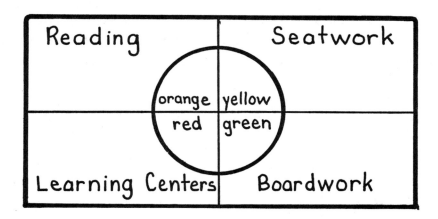

In this diagram, the orange group is working with me at the reading area, the yellow group is doing seatwork (math and phonics papers), the green group is at the boardwork area (copying some type of work from the chalkboard), and the red group is working at eight different learning centers (one child per learning center). At the end of one half hour, the color wheel is turned clockwise and all of the groups move to the next area. The groups continue to move in this way until each group has completed all four areas.

A makeup time (approximately 15 minutes) is given after the children have completed all four areas. This enables all of the children to finish their morning work. In the afternoon we have whole group activities: math, social studies, phonics, spelling, art, handwriting, and so on.

Participation in learning centers will be a new experience to many of our children. I have prepared activities for eight individual learning centers covering the following skills: math, art, social studies, science, reading, listening, handwriting, and coordination.

There are several reasons why I am teaching with learning centers: (1) The classroom is quieter; (2) a structured routine is followed daily; (3) the children learn to follow directions; (4) independent study habits are established; (5) the children can pace themselves to work for thirty minutes; (6) the children learn to evaluate themselves; and (7) a wide variety of subjects provides experiences in learning something new, reinforcing old skills, or developing creativity.

During the next eight school days the learning centers will be based on the theme _____. If you have books, records, or games about this learning center topic, please share them. (Please be sure that your child's name is on any item sent to school.) If you are interested in seeing our learning centers in action, please contact me to arrange an appointment. I am looking forward to seeing you.

The beginning weeks of learning centers may present some new adjustments. We will have a routine established within a week. Thank you for your support.

Sincerely,

_____

Your child's teacher

LEARNING CENTERS' EVENING MEETING

October _____

Dear Parent,

     Since many people are unable to visit the classroom during the school day, I would like to invite you and your child to a group meeting. The meeting will be held in Room _____ at the _____ School on _____ at _____ P.M. It will last approximately one hour.

     The meeting will consist of the following:

1. A brief presentation of the learning centers approach that we are using daily in our classroom.
2. A question-and-answer period.
3. An opportunity for you and your child to visit our room to see learning centers.

     I appreciate the support that you have given me this year. I would like to know how many people plan to attend the meeting. Please return the following note by _____.

Sincerely,

_____
Your child's teacher

- -

_____
Your child's name

Please check one of the following:

_____ We will be able to attend the meeting on _____.

            The number planning to attend is _____.

_____ We will not be able to attend the meeting.

_____
Parent's signature